CW00330579

YOUNG GUN

YOUNG GUN

THE BIOGRAPHY OF
CESC FÀBREGAS

TOM OLDFIELD

JOHN BLAKE

Published by John Blake Publishing Ltd,
3 Bramber Court, 2 Bramber Road,
London W14 9PB, England

www.johnblakepublishing.co.uk

First published in hardback in 2009

ISBN: 978-1-84454-642-8

British Library Cataloguing-in-Publication Data:

A catalogue record for this book is available from the British Library.

Design by www.envydesign.co.uk

Printed in the UK by CPI William Clowes, Beccles, NR34 7TL

1 3 5 7 9 10 8 6 4 2

Papers used by John Blake Publishing are natural, recyclable products
made from wood grown in sustainable forests. The manufacturing processes
conform to the environmental regulations of the country of origin.

For Mum and Dad
Thank you for the endless love, support
and encouragement

CONTENTS

INTRODUCTION

Cesc Fábregas' journey to the top in European football must be one of the fastest in history and it is an incredible story. Only just into his twenties, Fábregas has already featured in the Arsenal first team for five seasons, not to mention the 2006 World Cup and the glorious Euro 2008 campaign with his national team, Spain. With every passing week, his reputation as one of the planet's biggest talents grows and grows and there seems to be no limit to how far Cesc can progress in the game.

Few players have had such an impressive and immediate impact on English football during the Premiership era. Even fewer have achieved it at such a young age. Fábregas wasted little time in making his mark in the Arsenal first team and might just go down as the biggest gem Arsène Wenger has unearthed in his spell as Gunners boss. Cesc makes football look so easy, but while his rise to the top has been rapid, he has had to put in plenty of hard work and has taken some big, brave decisions along the way.

Born and raised in Barcelona, Cesc had football in his blood. The Catalan giants quickly noticed his talent and signed him for their youth system, aged just ten. Many would have settled for the life Fábregas enjoyed at Barça, but the young Spaniard had other ideas and, at sixteen, took the bold step of moving to Arsenal; when he got there, he found a language and a climate to which he was far from accustomed. It was a huge step for someone so young, but Fábregas has always been a boy in a hurry – he wanted first-team football at all costs.

At Arsenal, Cesc's promotion to the senior side was faster than he could ever have envisioned. Wenger, renowned for his ability to get the best out of young footballers, spotted Fábregas' faultless range of passing and knew immediately that Cesc had the potential to play in the Gunners' midfield for years to come. Never afraid to throw fledglings into the fray, Arsène handed Fábregas his full Arsenal debut in the Carling Cup against Rotherham. Cesc was still just sixteen years of age, but he gave a good account of himself and more appearances followed in the competition that year.

The 2004/05 season was the breakthrough campaign for Fábregas. After a superb display in the FA Community Shield, he became a regular in Wenger's squads and proved that, despite his slight build, he could handle the physical side of Premiership football. Cesc's reward was an FA Cup-winner's medal at the end of a campaign that marked him out as one of Europe's brightest young stars.

Since then, he has got better and better, taking on more responsibility within the side. When Patrick Vieira joined Juventus in the summer of 2005, Arsène had no qualms about handing Fábregas a regular berth in midfield, knowing that the Spaniard would not let him down. The Gunners had a bad Premiership run that campaign – just sneaking a fourth-place finish – but stormed to the Champions League final, eliminating powerhouses Juventus and Real Madrid along the way. Cesc and company were just minutes from lifting the trophy in Paris, only for Barcelona to turn things around in the latter stages.

There would be no summer break for Fábregas, though. He was selected for Spain's 2006 World Cup squad and set more records as he forced his way into the starting line-up during the tournament in Germany. On a personal note, it capped what had been a superb season. Spain may have been eliminated in the second round, but not before Cesc had shown the world why he was so highly rated.

The 2006/07 campaign saw Fábregas play a leading role as Arsenal moved into their new home, the Emirates Stadium. The team did not pick up any silverware, despite reaching the Carling Cup final, but the side's potential was there for all to see. Though Thierry Henry left the club in the summer of 2007, Fábregas remained upbeat about the Gunners' prospects. Still only twenty, he was ready for a more senior role in the team and was determined to add more medals to his collection. More silverware has not been forthcoming though at Arsenal as the club have fallen short of expectations, despite some superb moments in the 2007/8 campaign. However, Fabregas made his mark for Spain, winning Euro 2008, and he has since taken on the captain's armband at club level.

Within the space of a few seasons, Cesc has matured from a fledgling of the Gunners' squad into one of the team's leaders, and he has done so with the minimum of fuss. His range of passing, coupled with his understanding of his team-mates' runs, allows him to control the midfield areas and dictate the flow of matches. And he rarely falls short of the high standards he sets for himself. Fábregas is never shy to get into the opposition penalty area and he has even added goalscoring to his list of attributes – a major improvement on previous years.

With so many seasons ahead of him at the top, expect to see plenty more of Cesc Fábregas. For anyone who has watched him play over the past four years, that will come as a welcome relief.

CHAPTER 1
CHILDHOOD

Francesc Fábregas Soler was born on 4 May 1987 to parents Francesc senior and Nuria. Along with his sister Carlota, the family lived in Arenys de Mar in the Maresme county of Barcelona. The small town, with a population of around 14,000, is a major fishing port and it offered Cesc a relaxed environment. Family has always played an important part in Fábregas' life and he recalls his childhood fondly. His home town was away from the city centre, meaning that his days involved plenty of travel to and from school. But he did it. He never missed school.

As Cesc grew up, his father still ran the family construction business that has been passed down through generations. His mother, Nuria would go on to become a director of a sales company. Both have always been busy with their jobs, but time was always set aside for family meals and activities. They were a close-knit family and Cesc's parents have always been very supportive. They have taken great pride in the way their son has blossomed into a fine professional footballer and follow his career religiously, making trips to London whenever possible to see him in action.

It seems that a passion for football was in the genes for Cesc. Fábregas' father, Francesc senior, played the sport seriously in his youth and, though he did not make the grade in the way his son has done, he was clearly a useful footballer in his day. As an article in the *Evening Standard* explained: 'Francesc [senior] had a trial with Barcelona but was turned down and played for a Third Division team, Calella.' Obviously, there was no shortage of football conversations around the dinner table.

Growing up in Barcelona was every boy's dream: a beautiful city, a nice climate, gorgeous beaches and a hugely successful and entertaining football team. What more could Cesc have wanted? Unsurprisingly, it did not take long for Fábregas to develop a keen interest in the city's number one football club. The whole family were Barça fans so, in truth, he had little choice in the matter! They were season-ticket holders and so he was fortunate enough to sample the atmosphere inside the Nou Camp from a young age – certainly younger than most children are when they attend their first match. Rumour has it that Cesc was just nine months old when his grandfather Alex took him to the Nou Camp for the first time. Fábregas also recalls his first football kit, a Barcelona strip, one that he wore with great pride.

The Barça side played with a stylish swagger that he loved to watch and he was glued to the television at every opportunity. This is where he built his idealistic view of how the game should be played – with plenty of flair and no negative tactics. He saw Barcelona win the European

Cup against Sampdoria in 1992 and witnessed the jubilant celebrations that followed. Two years later, when he was still only seven, he watched as the club reached the 1994 Champions League final, only to see them lose 4-0 to AC Milan in a very one-sided contest. It taught him the highs and lows of football at a young age. Plenty more big occasions would follow.

He told *Arsenal TV Online* that he was probably around nine years old when he first heard of Arsenal Football Club and his memories of that team were the figures of Tony Adams and David Seaman. It is a reminder of just how young he is – those players had only recently ended their Arsenal careers when Fábregas joined the club yet he recalled watching them play at the age of just nine! It would not be fair to say, though, that he followed the Gunners with any keen interest – Barcelona was the only team he was interested in.

His favourite player at that time was Barça's Spanish midfielder Josep Guardiola, a classy passer of the ball on whom Cesc seems to have based aspects of his own game. Indeed, the fact that Fábregas now wears the number four shirt for Arsenal is a tribute to Guardiola, who wore the same number in his days at Barça. Guardiola himself, now Barcelona boss, would have been proud of many of his compatriot's displays in his recent seasons.

Fábregas still has a season ticket for the Nou Camp which he uses when he has time off at Arsenal. He has never thought of relinquishing it, preferring to loan it out to friends than give it up altogether. For Cesc, it is worth having the season ticket just for the few games he can attend each season. On the odd occasions that Wenger grants him time off, he likes nothing better than to go home and watch Barcelona play. His love for the team has not waned over the years: Barça will be his club for life.

Cesc has made occasional references to his schooldays. He revealed to *Arsenal TV Online* that was not a model pupil back then and anyone who has seen him play can picture a mischievous youngster with a rebellious streak. However, any trouble he caused was of a minor nature. He claimed he was cheeky at school and, while he got good marks in exams, his attitude may not always have been the best - and it resulted in him spending plenty of time standing outside the classroom. He has no regrets, though. 'Who has ever not done anything wrong? No one is a saint,' the Spaniard once said.

He played against boys several years older than him – as is often the way with good young footballers – and this toughened him up. The pitches were rarely of a good quality and falling regularly resulted in nasty cuts and bruises. You could call it a school of hard knocks. But Cesc relished the challenge of outwitting stronger opponents and it taught him the value of being a clever player as well as a skilful one. He learnt to find a pass quickly to avoid rough tackles, although he was not afraid to put his foot in himself. Even today, despite his relatively slight frame, it is noticeable that the Spaniard shows no fear in the tackle and he does his fair share of grafting in midfield. The feeling of being part of a team is important for all aspiring players and these formative years had a massive impact on the type of footballer Fábregas would become. He was a joy to watch and played the game in a way that pleased all football purists.

He struck up plenty of friendships during these informal

games. As one can imagine, Cesc's ability on the football pitch made him very popular and earned him the respect of the older boys, even if they did play in a more physical manner against him to prevent embarrassment. Fábregas was never happier than when he had a ball at his feet.

People soon started to take notice as he starred for local side Mataro. But even when he was attracting the attention of professional clubs, Cesc still thought his future lay in continuing the family construction firm. Such thought processes help explain why Fábregas never became arrogant about his rise to stardom and why to this day he has kept many of his childhood friends. As he explained in an interview with *The Sunday Times*: 'I love my friends because they've known me since I was small and treat me like always. They kid me, they make jokes.' It allows him to slip back into his old routine whenever he wants to.

In the same interview, Cesc admitted that part of the reason he was not always fixed on becoming a footballer came from his father, who was not 'one of those dads who goes crazy with their sons, saying "You have to be a footballer!"' He was under no pressure and his parents' laid-back approach allowed Fábregas to discover where his future lay by himself. He was encouraged to enjoy the beauty of the game because, first and foremost, he was told, football should be about having fun. Winning has always been extremely important to him as well, but it is a passion for the joys of attacking football that got Fábregas hooked on the sport. After all, he is in the entertainment business.

When Barcelona revealed their interest in signing Cesc for their youth system, it was a chance of a lifetime. He might not have set his heart on making the grade at this stage, but Fábregas knew a good opportunity when he saw one. Barça were such a big part of Cesc's life already and now he would be training with the club. He had to pinch himself to make sure it was not a dream. It was an overwhelming development for him – he was still only ten years old and he had the world at his feet.

Combining his studies with the training schedule at Barcelona proved tricky and gave Fábregas little time to himself. As he recalled in an interview with the *Daily Mail*: 'I had to wake up early in the morning, go to school, come back, have lunch, rest a little bit, go running, then a taxi was coming to pick up about six of us and take us to training at Barcelona. We would train at 7.30pm, finish at 9.30pm, take a taxi home again. Then I would have to do my homework, sometimes to 2am or 3am and wake up early again to go to school. It was like that for five years, really hard.' It was certainly a tough routine, but he thrived on those training sessions and they stood out as the highlight of his week. What's more, he was the envy of all his school friends.

The Barcelona youth set-up, or *cantera*, is world renowned for bringing through exceptionally gifted young footballers. It is something the club takes very seriously and managers and coaches feel great pride in unearthing special fledgling talents. For Fábregas to be invited to join the *cantera* was an indication that big things were expected of him. No end of fanatical youngsters may have dreamed of pulling on the Barcelona shirt, but it was Cesc who had been hand-picked by the club's scouts. It was a massive moment for him at such a young age and he just tried to give a good account of himself each week in training.

Set on the outskirts of Barcelona, the *cantera* put plenty of distance between training sessions and the temptations of the city. The list of players who have graduated from this system is lengthy and includes Lionel Messi, Xavi Hernandez, Andres Iniesta and Carlos Puyol (all now in the Barcelona first team), as well as Pepe Reina, the Liverpool goalkeeper, and Mikel Arteta, who has proved a revelation since his transfer to Everton. And, of course, in recent times a handful of youngsters from the *cantera*, including Bojan Krkic, who is receiving rave reviews across the country at present, have broken into, or are on the verge of breaking into, the Barça side on a regular basis.

Messi was one of the youngsters training in the set-up at the same time as Cesc and the little Argentine holds the Barcelona *cantera* in the highest esteem. As he told John Carlin in the *Observer Sport Monthly*: 'The Barcelona youth programme is one of the best in the world. As a kid they teach you not to play to win, so much as to grow in ability as a player. At Barça, we trained every day with the ball. I hardly ever ran without a ball at my feet. It was a form of training aimed very clearly at developing your skills.'

It is easy to understand how Fábregas became so composed and assured in possession of the ball. The group learned to play the 'Barcelona way' and it is noticeable that the styles of Cesc, Xavi and Iniesta are very similar. All three love to be on the ball and have an eye for a pass while gliding effortlessly around the pitch. Playing alongside such talented fledglings, Fábregas had to raise his game to keep up, but he has never been short of self-belief. It may occasionally come across as arrogance; Fábregas simply believes in his ability to win football games.

Matches for the Barcelona youth sides were generally heavily one-sided. Fábregas recalls the team picking up a string of emphatic victories with scorelines that sometimes resembled rugby results. Cesc and company certainly had no trouble finding the back of the net. With a monopoly on most of the hottest young talent in the region, if not the country, Barça were just too good for most of their opponents, even in these youth leagues.

The youth system taught Fábregas valuable lessons for football and for life. He was thankful that his family lived in the city and that he did not find himself isolated, as is the case with some young hopefuls. Cristiano Ronaldo, for instance, had to leave the island of Madeira behind when he moved to Sporting Lisbon and years of homesickness followed. Messi, too, was separated from family and friends during his time in the Barcelona academy after heading to Spain from Argentina. Cesc, though, had no such issues to worry him; it made things easier for him as he had no major distractions.

Many young hopefuls see the standard of their school work fall away as they pursue a career in football, but Fábregas showed equal commitment to his studies. Speaking to the *Daily Mail* in 2007, he revealed: 'I never did something like … how do you say? Truant. Maybe sometimes I was thinking about it, but I knew I would feel bad afterwards, so I never did it. In the end I got all my exams and good grades. Now I can speak Spanish, Catalan, English and a little bit of French.'

He had given himself the opportunity to live and play elsewhere in Europe and now had a 'Plan B' in case he needed to fall back on his education in due course. Not many young footballers can say the same, but Cesc had shown he was one step ahead, both on and off the pitch.

One of the benefits for big sports fans in countries such as Spain or Italy is the availability of newspapers devoted solely to sport and, in particular, to football. In England, such papers are scarce. Fábregas quickly became aware of these Spanish publications and read them avidly. The region of Catalonia produces two papers – *Sport* and *El Mundo Deportivo* – and they document the ins and outs of life at Barcelona while pouring scorn on any Real Madrid slip-ups. Their daily bulletins are designed precisely for fans such as Cesc.

Fábregas' next big moment came when he was selected in the Spanish squad for the FIFA Under-17 World Cup in Finland in 2003. It was a tremendous honour for him to represent his country and it was also a major step forward in his development. Cesc's progress at Barcelona had caught the eye of the team's selectors and his reputation was beginning to grow. The tournament offered exposure for young players in front of a worldwide audience, putting them in the shop window for top clubs. There were always plenty of scouts at such events, hoping to discover the 'next big thing' and, while Fábregas could not aim much higher than representing Barcelona, he wanted to impress the crowds nonetheless.

Knowledgeable Spanish supporters raved about Cesc's talent and had already earmarked him as a youngster who would have a long career in the senior side. Elsewhere, though, Fábregas was relatively unknown at this stage. The media attention came as something of a surprise to him; it was a new experience, as was the fact that each of Spain's games would be televised for fans back home. The players were frequently asked for autographs and Cesc was only too happy to oblige. He just hoped the team could live up to their expectations.

He need not have worried. Spain enjoyed a terrific tournament and Fábregas was central to their success, pulling the strings and popping up with a staggering number of goals from midfield – he collected the Golden Boot after finishing as the competition's top scorer with six goals. In the semi-final against Argentina, Cesc went head-to-head with Messi, his Barcelona colleague, in what proved to be a thrilling contest between two excellent sides. Spain were the victors in a gripping extra-time finale and Fábregas still recalls the match with great pride, telling *FIFA.com*: 'In that game we were 2-0 down in the first half, but we went on to win the game in the last minute of extra time. In football, everybody knows that in the space of five minutes a game can be turned completely on its head.' He and his team-mates were one match away from lifting the trophy.

Sadly, the Under-17 World Cup did not have a perfect ending for the Spaniards as they fell to a 2-0 defeat in the final against Brazil. It was the one low point of the tournament for Fábregas, but it made him even more determined to succeed next time. He had now experienced the pain of losing a showpiece final and did not want to feel that disappointment again in a hurry.

While team glory will always be Cesc's top priority, he was nonetheless delighted to be named the World Cup Golden Ball winner, awarded to the tournament's best player. It did not make up for missing out on the big prize, but it was some consolation, as he told *FIFA.com*:

'Winning an individual award is a great boost for your confidence. It's a great feeling to be recognised as the best player in a world championship.'

It had been a remarkable, even life-changing, spell for Fábregas. He returned to his club duties with renewed self-belief and a bigger appetite for success. The time in Finland had been wonderful and he would never forget the team's efforts there, but Cesc was ready to move on to the next stage of his career – wherever that might be.

He was enjoying his time at Barcelona and saw his game improve week by week. But he was realistic and questioned whether he would receive a first-team opportunity at the club, considering the enormous talent of the first team squad. He claims that even at this stage he did not think of himself as a professional footballer, yet his next decision would push him firmly in that direction.

Frustrated and concerned that he would be frozen out at Barcelona, Fábregas was uneasy. So strong were his ties to the club, he would not have considered moving if he saw any chance of progressing into the first team. The signs this would not happen for him must have been there. When Arsenal manager Arsène Wenger revealed his interest in bringing Cesc to London, it presented the youngster with a new possibility. It would mean plenty of upheaval, but Wenger seemed certain that Fábregas could make the grade in the Premiership. It was an attractive proposition and, in the end, Cesc felt he could not turn it down.

It was certainly not an easy decision and, naturally, Fábregas had doubts about the move. He told the media: 'At Barça, we played Arsenal a few months before in a youth tournament and we beat them 5-1. I scored two goals and I was like, "I don't want to go because we are better." But then they made me the proposal and I saw that Arsenal was a great club. I came to see the training ground and to talk to Mr Wenger. Imagine, you are playing Under-16s at Barcelona and then you are talking to a person like Arsène Wenger, who is so important in this world of football. It impressed me a lot. I had something in my mind saying, "Go on, you have to sign because everything is going to be fine."'

The coaches at Barça were distraught to hear the news. It came as a shock that someone had flown the nest but, though they have since tightened up their attempts to keep youngsters happy at the club, there have since been two other exits – Gerard Pique to Manchester United and, most recently, Fran Merida to Arsenal. Naturally, a team like Barcelona were not used to the notion of players wanting to leave – after all, who would want to move away from such a famous set-up? But Cesc had bucked that particular trend.

In May 2006, Barcelona president Joan Laporta made his feelings clear on the matter. It was easy to see his frustration. Barça were pouring funding into their youth system, but were then losing the products of this set-up to other clubs. If Barcelona could not hang on to their top youngsters it made all the nurturing and guidance worthless; and it was especially irritating when these fledglings moved to Champions League rivals such as Arsenal and Manchester United. But there was little the president could do.

Laporta was quoted in the *Independent* as saying: 'We are a club that has invested €7 million in our youth team this season. But we have a big problem with English clubs who are targeting our youngsters. Before they used to do it with French clubs and now it seems as though we are next. The British clubs offer astronomical figures to kids who are fourteen, fifteen and sixteen, a figure that we cannot equal. We had this situation with Cesc Fábregas, Gerard Pique and now with Fran Merida.' Clearly, time had not healed the wounds at Barça. The club's officials had tried to persuade Cesc to stay, but his mind was made up.

And so, in July 2003, Fábregas completed his move from Barcelona to Arsenal. At just sixteen years of age, it was a brave decision. He had concerns over whether he might regret walking away from one of the biggest clubs in the world, but they paled in comparison to his desire to further his career. He was arriving in a new country and it would take time for him to adjust to the culture and language. Wenger did his best to help the youngster settle and Cesc took the changes in his stride. Leaving Barcelona behind had been difficult – they were his boyhood team and it was his home city – but in time he would have confirmation that it had been a career defining switch.

He has since revealed that a number of his team-mates in the Barcelona youth teams did not progress much further and had not been given a chance in the first team. Fábregas had chosen not to take that gamble, preferring the more promising option of linking up with Wenger in London. Football can be such a cruel business and Cesc was seemingly aware of the heartbreak that might be ahead of him had he stayed at Barça. The decision to move to Arsenal also brings into question the youngster's claims that he never thought about making the grade in football. Surely, swapping Spain for England was a switch designed essentially to improve his chances of becoming a professional footballer –

as usual, Fábregas has been too modest about his early ambitions.

His family was delighted for him, although it meant he would be out of their lives for long periods. They spoke often on the telephone in the early Arsenal days and, of course, because the journey from Barcelona to London is now relatively quick, simple and inexpensive, his home town was never too far away. But it was tough for Cesc to leave his girlfriend, Carla, behind when he headed to England. Fortunately, he has never been short of self-confidence and this was vital in the first six months in England as he strove to adapt to the new surroundings and the absence of his loved ones.

The club arranged accommodation for Cesc when he arrived in North London. He and Philippe Senderos, the Swiss central defender, lived with an Irish landlady called Noreen. Fábregas still goes back to visit her from time to time. She helped the pair come to terms with the English lifestyle and gave them a safe, happy base in which to relax away from their football commitments. It was exciting to be able to take in the sights of London on a regular basis and, as he became more confident, Cesc spent more time exploring the city.

One of the nice things about Fábregas is that he has always been grateful to Arsenal for giving him the chance to become a first team player. From the moment he arrived in the English capital, Cesc has shown himself to be thankful for his opportunity. It is something that so many other youngsters take for granted – as if it is their divine right to become a professional footballer.

Former Arsenal defender Martin Keown tells a funny story from Fábregas' early days at the club. He explained in the *Sunday Mirror*: 'I remember meeting his [Cesc's] mother and she was about the same age as me. I thought, "It's about time to get out now! When you're older than your team-mate's mother, the writing is definitely on the wall!"' For the veterans in the Arsenal squad, it must have been staggering to see the club bringing such young footballers into the set-up. In their day, players of nineteen or twenty years of age were considered bright young things. Now teams were looking to recruit players as young as fifteen or sixteen.

Nuria worried a lot in the early months about whether her son would cope with the switch. And while she tried to visit as often as she could, it did not always calm her nerves. Fábregas recalls: 'When I first came over, my mother was a little worried and her first question every time she phoned was about whether I was eating properly. Like every mother, she worries, but she is fine now.'

Learning to speak English fluently was one of the toughest challenges Fábregas faced but, just as with his football, he soon made progress. He was aided by the large number of Spanish speakers in the Arsenal squad – Robert Pires, Manuel Almunia and later Jose Antonio Reyes – who made life easier for him, but Fábregas had to grow up very quickly. He did not enjoy the freedom teenagers usually have and he never succumbed to the typical teenage temptations. He once had a puff of a cigarette at his church confirmation, but only because it was a family tradition. He has not taken the cigarettes and drugs route and does not drink alcohol very often. There was no teenage rebellion. He preferred the quiet life.

At sixteen, he expected to work his way up through the youth system over the next few seasons then step up to the first team when he had matured. There was no pretence: he was ready to serve a long apprenticeship if that's what it took to make his mark at the club. Wenger had other ideas, though, and Fábregas soon realised that the remainder of his journey to first-team football would be far shorter than he could ever have imagined.

The coaching staff at Arsenal had told Cesc in no uncertain terms which areas of his game he needed to improve. Speaking to the *Independent*, Fábregas looked back to his formative years at the club and revealed how he was encouraged to work on the defensive elements of his game: 'They [Arsenal] just told me when I came here, "OK we signed you because you are good technically, but if you don't defend you cannot play for Arsenal." That's why I had to achieve that and I showed the manager I could do it. You have to believe in yourself. When they told me that, I believed I could do it.'

In the meantime, though, he concentrated on impressing in the Under-17 side, which was packed with talented youngsters who, as was the case at Barcelona, were all comfortable in possession of the ball. Wenger had ensured that his hallmark playing style was taught at all levels. Fábregas remembers those early days well, telling the *Daily Mail*: 'My very first match for Arsenal was against Coventry, away, in the Under-17s. My family came and it was freezing cold. My dad came, my grandparents, two uncles and two aunts and they were all freezing as well.' It was hardly an auspicious start, but things soon improved, even if the weather did not.

His performances for the Under-17s caught the eye of the coaching staff and he began to feature for the reserves, too. He was still very slight and would need to bulk up considerably to cope with Premiership football, but his talent was unquestionable. As tends to be the case at football clubs, whispers began to spread about an exciting young Spaniard who was progressing through the ranks at a rapid pace.

Cesc watched on as the Gunners marched towards an unbeaten league season in 2003/04. The likes of Thierry Henry, Robert Pires and Patrick Vieira produced incredible consistency along the way and few could dispute the quality of the side as they swept all before them – champions Manchester United had no reply. Fábregas did all he could to learn from his more experienced colleagues and every minute with them taught him more about how to reach the top of the game. The way the players looked after their bodies gave him an example to follow; their decision-making was something he hoped to emulate.

While he did not feature in the Premiership, Cesc was given opportunities to shine in the Carling Cup – a competition in which Wenger has always looked to blood the youngsters in his squad in order to examine their first-team credentials and their rate of progression. Fábregas made his Arsenal debut at home to Rotherham on 28 October 2003 in the third round of the Carling Cup. While he may have been unknown to many in the stadium, his performance on the night made plenty take note. Sporting the number fifty-seven shirt, Cesc helped Arsenal take the lead through Jeremie Aliadiere and, when he was substituted, the Gunners looked on course for a 1-0 victory. But a late equaliser for Rotherham forced extra-time and then penalties, with Arsenal grabbing a narrow 9-8 triumph. Fábregas watched nervously from the sidelines, praying that his team-mates made no mistake from 12 yards.

For the youngsters, progress in the Carling Cup meant more chances to impress Wenger. The Frenchman made it clear that the fledglings would continue to get the nod in the competition's future rounds and this offered extra incentives for those involved. A few big performances might convince the club to think about extending players' contracts and Cesc wanted to be at the forefront of his manager's mind when such decisions were being made.

He had to wait until 2 December for his next taste of the action. The Carling Cup fourth-round draw paired the Gunners with Wolverhampton Wanderers, again at Highbury. Wenger kept his promise to test out some of his younger players, selecting Cesc in a midfield berth alongside Patrick Vieira. To play alongside his club captain was a special moment for the young Spaniard and, desperately seeking to impress, he certainly made the most of it. Vieira helped Cesc throughout the game, giving advice and encouragement, just as he did on the training ground.

Arsenal led 1-0 at half-time, but really turned on the style after the interval and three goals in eleven minutes made it a comfortable finish for the Gunners. Wolves pulled a goal back before Fábregas enjoyed perhaps the most memorable moment of his career. In the right place at the right time, Cesc stabbed home a loose ball with two minutes to go. It was his first goal for the club and was rightly met with loud applause. Wenger was delighted with Fábregas' display and, back home, Cesc's family beamed with pride.

It was a special night but Fábregas did not celebrate in the way some youngsters might have done. Admittedly he was not yet of drinking age anyway but, as Cesc told the *Guardian*, he opted for a Coke and a Kinder Egg to savour the moment. It is a reminder of just how quickly he had burst onto the scene. Most people his age had only finished their GCSEs that summer; he was playing in front of more than 28,000 people at Highbury. It must have been difficult for his mates at home to come to terms with just how far their friend had progressed. They were all proud of him and chatted regularly with him over the internet to hear his latest news and fill him in on their latest adventures. This was important for Cesc too, as it stopped him from feeling isolated away from his family and childhood friends. The people back home were only a phone call or a click of a button away.

Fábregas had played well enough to feel legitimately disgruntled at the decision to drop him to the bench for the Carling Cup quarter-final away to West Brom on 16 December. It was all part of the learning process for Cesc. Wenger introduced Fábregas with just over fifteen minutes remaining. The Gunners were already 2-0 ahead and it was simply a case of closing out the contest. Victory meant another chance to shine as Arsenal looked forward to a semi-final with Middlesbrough.

Middlesbrough and Arsenal faced each other four times in less than a month in the New Year. While the Gunners dominated the Premiership and FA Cup clashes, winning both games 4-1, Boro enjoyed success in the Carling Cup bouts. Sadly for Fábregas, he did not take part in either contest and the second-string line-up missed his assured passing in midfield. Trailing 1-0 after the first leg, Wenger threw a few more first-team players into the return match, but it was not to be. Middlesbrough won

3-1 on aggregate and Cesc was denied the possibility of appearing in a showpiece final.

The Gunners soon had the Premiership title wrapped up, but their bid for an unbeaten league season persuaded Wenger not to throw his youngsters into league action. In other circumstances, Arsène would surely have handed Fábregas a few Premiership starts in the final few weeks of the campaign to pick up valuable experience. Instead, the regulars were given the chance to finish what they had started and, after a 2-1 win on the last day of the campaign against Leicester, Arsenal could celebrate going through an entire Premiership season without defeat. It was a remarkable achievement that left Fábregas eager to play alongside the big names. He had already learned so much from working with Arsène and the stars in the Gunners squad. Now he wanted to be part of the action on a more regular basis.

Cesc spent the summer reflecting on the incredible progress he had made during the 2003/04 campaign. It had been a superb season: making his Arsenal debut, scoring his first goal for the club, playing alongside Patrick Vieira. Fábregas could never have expected to rise through the ranks so quickly, but Wenger's eye for quality had been spot on yet again. Little did Cesc know that Arsène would have much bigger plans for his diminutive Spaniard when the 2004/05 campaign kicked off. When August came round, Fábregas would be thrown in at the deep end, but once again he would serve notice of his prodigious talent.

CHAPTER 2

BURSTING ONTO
THE SCENE

Fábregas had worked hard during the summer to ensure he was in peak condition for the new campaign and was rewarded with more involvement with the first-team squad on match days. Coming into the season with fresh legs meant he had an advantage over the international players who had been at Euro 2004 and Cesc noticed this during the early training sessions. As he claimed: 'You do need rest when you are so young and you start playing under a lot of pressure, especially in midfield where you have to run a lot and make a lot of tackles.' The break put him on top of his game when the pre-season preparation began.

The excitement of the 'Invincibles' season was still in the air and the club's supporters speculated as to how long the Gunners could keep up their unbeaten league record. Cesc, who had watched from afar as Arsenal overcame all before them, would now be in more regular contact with the heroes of that year. There was plenty of pressure on the players – could they possibly produce a campaign to rival the previous one?

There was limited transfer activity for the Gunners over the summer months and this caused some concern among those who wanted to see big-name signings. Wenger seemed happy to put his faith in the talented youngsters coming through the youth system and, of course, there was Reyes, who had only arrived from Sevilla in January and so was still adjusting to life in the Premiership. It was a boost for Fábregas that his manager had so much confidence in his young charges and he hoped this meant he would have a chance to force his way into Wenger's plans.

The worry for Arsenal fans was that their rivals had invested heavily during the summer in order to try to close the gap and stop a repeat of the 2003/04 rout. Cesc had no doubts over the ability within the Gunners squad, but he could understand why there were raised eyebrows over the lack of new faces at the club. Manchester United had announced their intention to win back the title by signing teenage sensation Wayne Rooney from Everton. The deal was worth an initial £20 million, with the possibility of another £7 million in the future. Chelsea also looked menacing and more resilient than had been the case in past campaigns. Roman Abramovich, the club's owner, had replaced manager Claudio Ranieri with Jose Mourinho and the new Blues boss had wasted little time in making his mark, particularly in front of the media. There were a string of new arrivals, including Arjen Robben and Didier Drogba.

Nonetheless, Fábregas was confident. It remained to be seen how many appearances he would make over the course of the season, but he looked around the team and felt sure the Gunners could defend their title. There was a perfect blend of experience and youth – he was joined in the first team by fellow fledglings, including new Dutch forward Robin van Persie. After all, it was a very long time since anyone had beaten Arsenal in the Premiership and there were plenty of assured figures in the dressing room. The big concern – and this would become an ongoing saga – was over Patrick Vieira's future. The Frenchman had clearly been tempted by an offer from Real Madrid and could not make up his mind over whether or not he wanted to stay at Highbury. It made it difficult for the team to plan for the campaign ahead and Vieira seemed troubled by the situation.

The FA Community Shield – previously the Charity Shield – has rarely been seen as a game to provide clues on the season ahead. It is merely seen a curtain raiser, nothing more. Yet the 2004 Community Shield clash between champions Arsenal and rivals Manchester United was an entirely different affair. It showed just how bright the Gunners' future would be as Wenger unleashed several talented youngsters in front of a large television audience for the first time.

Fábregas was delighted to be named in the starting line-up for the match at the Millennium Stadium in Cardiff. Surrounded by fellow fledglings, it would be a big test of the club's next generation and Cesc wanted to show that he belonged out there. Wenger had no qualms about throwing his youngsters into the fray against Roy Keane and company. And they did not let him down. They turned on the style in a breath-taking display of pace and movement to leave United shell-shocked as the

Gunners completed a comprehensive 3-1 victory. It confirmed that Arsenal were the best team in the country, and that they had the makings of a dynasty.

With Vieira's future uncertain, Cesc stepped into the Frenchman's role in midfield and gave a very assured performance, pinging the ball around. While Fábregas' compatriot Jose Antonio Reyes was the star of the show, his own efforts did not escape his manager's notice. Wenger told the press: 'To play like he did against a team of United's quality at seventeen is fantastic.' As Michael Hart observed in the *Evening Standard*: 'Fábregas, just seventeen and given the task of deputising for Vieira, played with such composure, thought and maturity to suggest he will develop into an outstanding midfield player.'

Those who watched Fábregas that afternoon will have noticed his eye-catching hairstyle. Sporting a mullet, Cesc ensured that it was not just his passing that made his performance memorable. It comes as little surprise that soon after Fábregas decided the mullet had to go! And he has kept his hair shorter ever since.

Another interesting element of the Community Shield clash was a chant the Arsenal fans created for Fábregas – the new kid on the block. Using the tune of a Vieira verse, the Gunners' supporters sang: 'He's only seventeen, he's better than Roy Keane.' It was a special moment for Cesc and it was certainly not the last time the chant would be brought out. The Spaniard explained his views on the match to the media: 'I love it when they sing that song. I don't think I'm better than Roy Keane for a minute, but it gives me a nice feeling when I hear it.'

As the 2004/05 league season began, it was clear that Cesc had convinced Wenger that he was ready to step up to the first team on a regular basis. At just seventeen years and 103 days old, Fábregas became the youngest Premiership debutant in the club's history. Taking his league bow away to Everton at Goodison Park, Cesc impressed everyone as he helped his team-mates achieve a comfortable 4-1 victory and the quality of his performance disguised any nerves he may have felt.

Far from being overawed by the occasion, he was prominent in midfield and absent captain Vieira was hardly missed. It provided Gunners fans with a glimpse into the club's future – and the fate of the team was clearly in capable hands. Cesc did not get on the scoresheet himself, but his probing passing sparked wave after wave of Arsenal attacks. Dennis Bergkamp, Jose Antonio Reyes, Freddie Ljungberg and Robert Pires may have grabbed the goals, but it was Fábregas who stole all the headlines. For the second week in a row, everyone was talking about him.

Wenger was immensely proud of his fledgling midfielder, telling the press: 'Francesc Fábregas is only seventeen, but age is not important. We had a seventeen-year-old and a thirty-five-year-old in Dennis Bergkamp and they both showed that age does not matter. As long as you have intelligence and technique, then that is enough.' This philosophy would serve the club very well over the next few years.

Cesc was flattered by the praise, but resolved to keep his feet on the ground. He knew he had a long way to go in terms of establishing himself at the top level and only had to look around the Arsenal dressing room to remind himself of it. Surrounded by players of the quality of Bergkamp, Henry and Vieira, Fábregas had no time to become complacent. These experienced players had plenty of know-how for the Spaniard to tap into. They had won the biggest honours in the game and were excellent role models for young footballers. The advice the youngster received from this group of seasoned pros must have been of enormous benefit.

Wenger promised to protect Fábregas from the rigours of the English fixture list, but indicated that the Spaniard would see many more first-team minutes over the course of the campaign. After the Everton game, Arsène explained: 'He is good enough to be a regular now. It is about finding the right balance, but I wanted to open the door for the young talent at the club.'

While Everton boss David Moyes was frustrated by his side's defensive woes, he could not fault Arsenal's clinical finishing. He was no doubt impressed by Fábregas' contribution. With Vieira injured and Gilberto Silva substituted at Goodison Park due to a back problem, Cesc looked set for an extended run in the team.

The match against Everton was a huge breakthrough in Fábregas' short career to date. Facing fiery midfielders Thomas Gravesen and Lee Carsley – dubbed 'the Mitchell brothers' – he stood up to the physicality of the contest. Wearing the number fifteen shirt after Ray Parlour's exit in the summer, Cesc played like a veteran and when fans settled down to watch *Match of the Day* that night, they saw the emergence of a new talent.

Question marks remained over how often Wenger would use the youngster, especially considering the other stars in the Arsenal squad. But the Frenchman showed a lot of faith in Fábregas, selecting him in the starting line-up again for the home game against Middlesbrough. This was partly due to injuries, but it was also a reward for the Spaniard's stellar form. The clash with Boro was a terrific contest, dominated by attacking football, and Cesc helped the Gunners recover from 3-1 down to win 5-3. The victory stretched Arsenal's unbeaten league run to forty-two games and, in the process, equalled Nottingham Forest's long-standing record. Cesc was pleased with his performance and loved being part of the feast of attacking football. His pass had set up Bergkamp for the team's second goal and he was also involved in Pires' equaliser. In short, he had been at the heart of the comeback.

While it might have seemed natural for Wenger to rest Cesc in the midweek game against Blackburn, the Gunners boss did no such thing. Fábregas again proved pivotal as Arsenal eventually broke down a stubborn Rovers side. The youngster missed a decent chance in the first half, but was at the heart of all good things in the second period, helping to engineer the opener with an exquisite to pass to Bergkamp, who set up Henry. Gilberto made it 2-0, but replays suggested that the last touch came off Fábregas, but being new to the first team, Cesc did not protest too much about not being credited with the goal. His compatriot Reyes sealed the 3-0 victory. Nine points out of nine was a super start as the Gunners carried on where they had left off the previous season – only now there was a new maestro in midfield. It had been a great start to the season: Arsenal had gone past Forest's record and sat proudly at the top of the table.

Fábregas' form prompted journalist Ian Hughes to write an article entitled 'Fábregas the fabulous' on the BBC Sport website. Hughes claimed: 'Arsenal's Spanish teenager has been sensational in the opening games of the season. Especially when you consider that most seventeen-year-olds would be polishing rather than filling Patrick Vieira's boots.' In the same piece, Bob Wilson, the former Arsenal goalkeeper, added his verdict: 'From everything I've seen and everything I've heard about him, it is clear that Fábregas is going to be an absolutely massive, massive player. He is another diamond that Arsène Wenger has unearthed. I think Fábregas is one of the best young players there has ever been.'

Arsène joined in the praise, explaining to the press how impressive Cesc's performances had been thus far: 'He has been up against Thomas Gravesen, Ray Parlour and Tugay – three men. And in every game, he has done very well. That is something amazing. It is not stupid to think that he could be called up for the Spain first team. They have a lot of midfielders, but they should not be scared to take him. He has been consistent, his work-rate and commitment are outstanding, and his football is a joy to watch.'

The youngster could not have wished for a more favourable assessment of his first few appearances and felt proud of the way he had handled these occasions.

Training with Wenger had introduced Fábregas to interesting new approaches and the more sessions he spent with Arsène, the more he learnt about the game. The Frenchman left nothing to chance with his flawless preparation and the team had a state of the art training set-up at London Colney, complete with outdoor pitches, gyms, treatment areas and even a hydrotherapy pool. Wenger played a huge role in helping Cesc's body develop at the right pace, using supplements and other revolutionary approaches to get the best results. From short pep talks to specific stretching exercises, Arsène has made a science out of football management and this was exactly what Fábregas needed. His manager's intense competitiveness was a good match with the Spaniard's own mentality and Cesc felt confident he would fill his trophy cabinet while working with Wenger.

Arsène's ideas had been revolutionary when he first arrived in England in 1996, but since then he had won over those who had initially doubted him. The likes of Tony Adams and Ian Wright had been sceptical, but had since praised the impact of Wenger's approaches as a key reason for the Gunners' return to the glory days. Now another generation of Arsenal players were benefiting and Fábregas could immediately feel the improvements in both his fitness and his displays.

His meals were carefully regulated by the club and he received good advice on which foods to eat and which ones to avoid. Cesc spoke to the *Daily Mail* in November 2007 and thought back to how much of an impact Wenger's ideas had had on his diet: 'I eat a lot of pasta with tomato sauce. And then fish. The best is when we go to the Four Seasons Hotel in Canary Wharf before games and they give us potatoes, fish, chicken, pasta, eggs. I love it. But I have to admit that sometimes when I have a day off I like to go to the Krispy Kreme doughnut shop.' Arsène had certainly helped the players to take better care of their bodies, though doughnuts were probably not part of Wenger's advice!

A trip to Norwich on 28 August gave Fábregas his fourth consecutive league start. His sudden rise to the first team had taken him a little by surprise, but he was taking full advantage of his chance to shine. More glorious attacking football allowed the Gunners to cruise to a 4-1 victory as four different players got on the scoresheet. Cesc was not one of them, but he passed the ball accurately and was looking more and more at home in the centre of midfield. Sixteen goals in four games proved Arsenal were as rampant as ever.

Such was Fábregas' progress he now had international commitments to consider as he continued to shine for the Spanish Under-21 side and his displays marked him out as an exceptional young talent. Iñaki Sáez, then just starting out as the coach of the team, was well aware of Cesc's ability, telling *Marca* newspaper that he had followed the youngster's development for several years. On 7 September 2004, in Sáez's first game as Under-21 coach, Cesc played an important role, coming on as a substitute in a 2-0 victory against Bosnia. *Marca* newspaper noted the improvements in the Spanish side's display after the introduction of Fábregas and admired the youngster's understanding with Barcelona's Andres Iniesta, a fellow *cantera* product. Sáez was delighted, telling the press: 'To start with a win away from home always gives security for the future.' Cesc added his opinion after the match: 'It was a game that was difficult for us to open up because they are a very tough team. But we always dominated it. We deserved the victory without doubt.' Fábregas was enjoying international football and meeting up with his fellow youngsters. Eventually, though, he hoped to step up to the senior squad and experience the biggest stage of all – the World Cup. He just had to get his head down and keep working hard.

Back at Arsenal, Cesc eventually got a rest on 11 September as Vieira returned from injury against Fulham. Fábregas accepted that Wenger was probably right to give him a break from the action but, being young, he did not feel the signs of tiredness setting in. He told the media: 'Of course I like to play football and I will never say "no" when I am asked to play because I love it so much.' Three goals in nine second-half minutes wrapped up the points for Arsenal against the Cottagers and Fábregas made a brief cameo with the game already effectively over. At the moment, the Gunners were making everything look so simple and their unbeaten league run showed no signs of being brought to an end. It was just a question of how many they would score and it was a depressing sight for the rest of the Premiership, giving little hope to Manchester United and the rest of the title hopefuls. All over the pitch, Fábregas and his colleagues were looking assured. Would Arsenal finally be able to win back-to-back league crowns?

In midweek, Cesc's focus turned to the Champions League as the club began their campaign. Drawn in Group E alongside PSV Eindhoven, Rosenborg and Panathinaikos, Fábregas knew that top spot ought to be a formality, but there would be no complacency. A 1-0 triumph at home to PSV on 14 September was a solid start, even if the contest was ultimately decided by an own goal. Fábregas was an unused substitute that night, though, and would have to wait for his first taste of European football.

On 17 September, Cesc was finally able to put pen to paper and signed a contract with the Gunners until 2009. English law meant he had not been able to do so before, but he was only too happy to commit to the club, telling the media: 'My first year here has been like a dream. I never thought I would have the opportunity to play in the first team so soon. I am very excited for my future.' He wanted to give something back to the club that had given him his big chance in the limelight.

Wenger was equally pleased the Spaniard had committed to Arsenal: 'He is important for the future of the club. Cesc has shown a great maturity since he arrived, he has adapted very well to the English game. He has great vision and all the necessary characteristics to be a great player for us.' The Frenchman had seen enough already to know that Fábregas had a very bright future.

It was a big moment for the youngster and gave him financial security, knowing that the club had invested in his future. There was no doubt now – Arsenal would be the club where he blossomed into a top-class talent.

The next few weeks were a little subdued as Cesc had to accept a fringe role. He did not complain – after all, he was still young and had received assurances from Wenger over his future at the club. Instead, Fábregas watched intently and tried to pick up as much useful information as he could from the senior players. Even though they were not on top form, the Gunners refused to be beaten. A 2-2 draw at home to Bolton was followed by a 1-0 win at Manchester City and a 1-1 draw in Europe against Rosenborg. While the Spaniard did not feature much during this period, he received a boost when Vieira told the media how important Cesc was to the team, adding: 'The boy is incredible.' Perhaps the Frenchman was already predicting that Fábregas would be the man to replace him at Arsenal.

On 2 October, Wenger restored Fábregas to the starting line-up, giving him the chance to impress at Highbury against Charlton. While Cesc put in another promising shift, it was Henry who stole the show as he scored twice – one of which was an audacious backheel into the bottom corner. Fábregas was quickly becoming a firm favourite with the Arsenal supporters and the Spaniard loved the atmosphere inside the stadium on match days. His season was progressing better than he could have possibly anticipated and his body seemed to be holding up against the physical nature of English football.

His solid display ensured he kept his place for the visit of Aston Villa two weeks later. Cesc again fitted in perfectly with the pass-and-move football the Gunners loved to play and a 3-1 win did not tell the whole story of Arsenal's dominance. Fábregas never seemed to waste the ball or make the type of rash decisions one might expect from a youngster. He always knew where his team-mates were and found them with unerring accuracy. Much of that was down to his education at the Barcelona *cantera* where technique and passing were essential qualities and those training exercises, now that he had been given a first team opportunity at Arsenal, were serving him well.

The Spaniard was pleased to get his first Champions League outing under his belt in midweek against Panathinaikos. A 2-2 draw was a satisfactory result, but the Gunners failed to unleash their full artillery of attacking football. Fábregas was paired with Edu in midfield and the duo complemented each other well. Some nervy defending and a lapse from Jens Lehmann cost Arsenal two points that night in Greece. It was an eye-opening experience for the youngster as he saw the differences between football in the Champions League and the Premiership. Invariably, the Gunners found it much tougher to play their flowing passing game in Europe.

Keeping to his promise to look after Cesc's young body, Wenger named Fábregas among the substitutes for the trip to Old Trafford for a massive clash with Manchester United. If Arsenal avoided defeat, they would reach the incredible tally of fifty games unbeaten in the league. It was amazing that the computer had served up the contest at this point on the fixture list!

Naturally, United were desperate to be the team to deny the Gunners that record and the match simmered throughout. Fábregas was a little disappointed not to be out on the pitch, but he understood the decision. Vieira was available again and the Frenchman's presence always made a massive difference to the confidence within the team, particularly in big games. Cesc crossed his fingers that he would get a chance to impress off the bench at some stage.

A tight, physical contest ended in misery for Arsenal as United won 2-0. Wenger had opted not to use Fábregas at all that afternoon, but the youngster was just as annoyed as his team-mates about the scoreline. There was plenty of controversy over the penalty referee Mike Riley awarded against Sol Campbell for a challenge on Wayne Rooney in the seventy-third minute of the game. Contact seemed to be minimal and it just made the

Gunners – already furious at the rough treatment dished out to Reyes – even angrier. Ruud van Nistelrooy scored from the spot and Rooney added a second late on as Arsenal threw men forward.

This was only the start of the drama. Fábregas and his team-mates' frustration at losing their unbeaten record against United spilled over in the tunnel after the match. There have been various reports claiming to know what happened that day. It seems there was a fracas and that, amid the pushing and shoving, an Arsenal player hurled a piece of pizza that hit Sir Alex Ferguson in the face.

In Ashley Cole's autobiography, *My Defence*, the left-back also hit out at the Arsenal set-up and made a couple of harsh comments about Fábregas, his former team-mate. Incredibly, Cole called Cesc an 'unproven featherweight'. It was a comment the Spaniard chose to ignore.

The bottom line after the events at Old Trafford, though, was that Arsenal had lost. Their unbeaten streak was over and, to make matters worse, Fábregas and his team-mates appeared unable to come to terms with the defeat. The hangover from the loss sent the Gunners' season spiralling out of control. For some reason, Wenger and his players appeared to take defeat more ungraciously than other sides and Ferguson branded them 'the worst losers of all time.' From players surrounding the referee and protesting at decisions on the pitch to bitter post-match interviews, Arsenal were not winning themselves many friends. Wenger's reluctance to criticise any of his players led to questions over whether there was sufficient discipline within the Gunners set-up.

From leading the Premiership and looking imperious, Cesc and company suffered a worrying dip. It was hard for anyone connected with the club to put their finger on what had changed or what was going wrong, but fixtures against weaker sides suddenly became trickier than usual. It was all very annoying, but the Spaniard and the rest of his Arsenal colleagues were pleased to relieve some of their Old Trafford frustration with a 2-1 midweek victory over Manchester City in the Carling Cup.

Sloppiness marred the last game of October and then the entire month of November for the Gunners. A 2-2 draw with Southampton on 30 October saw Arsenal drop more important points and they needed a van Persie equaliser to keep them at the top of the table. Two goals from Rory Delap almost earned the Saints a shock win. Fábregas, on as a second-half substitute, could do little to stop the panic that was spreading through the back four. The Gunners had become rattled and seemed unable to hold onto leads.

November began with a 1-1 draw at home to Panathinaikos. The Gunners' ruthless streak had deserted them. Usually so prolific at home, many predicted the floodgates would open once Henry handed them the lead from the penalty spot, but Arsenal failed to put the game beyond their opponents. Despite Fábregas' excellent showing in midfield, the home side struggled. The visitors missed a great chance to equalise when they won a penalty of their own. Angelos Basinas fired over from the spot. Panathinaikos eventually draw level with fifteen minutes remaining as Pascal Cygan inadvertently deflected a long-range shot past Lehmann. Cesc, one of the few stars who lived up to his billing, could not believe the team's bad luck. After months and months of plain sailing, in the space of a few weeks the Gunners found themselves in choppy waters.

36

Another draw, this time away to Crystal Palace on 6 November, did little to lift the gloom in the Gunners camp. Fábregas began the move that put Arsenal ahead just after the hour mark, finding Ljungberg who crossed for Henry. But defensive wobbles proved costly again. Without Sol Campbell, the back four looked more vulnerable and Palace equalised just minutes later. The result gave plenty of encouragement to the rest of the Premiership and Chelsea, taking advantage of the Gunners' rotten form, ended the day two points clear at the top of the table.

After Arsenal's youngsters beat Everton 3-1 in the Carling Cup – Fábregas was rested as a reward for his good form – the first-team regulars recorded an incredible 5-4 victory over Tottenham in the North London derby to lift the mood around the club. It was one of the most enthralling matches of Cesc's short career. After going 3-1 up, the Gunners should have sealed the match, but again defensive frailties were exposed. Cygan, Campbell's replacement, was struggling to adapt to English football and opposition teams sensed that the back four were a shadow of their former selves. Panic quickly spread through the team and Fábregas and company just about managed to hang on for a much-needed three points. Cesc had laid on the third goal for Ljungberg and he stood up well in the heated atmosphere. The only worry was the team's inability to hold on to leads. As several wags put it, you would not let the Gunners walk your dog!

The hangover from the defeat to United in October continued as Arsenal drew 1-1 with West Brom at Highbury on 20 November. Jose Mourinho could not believe his luck as Chelsea stretched their lead at the top. A late goal from Rob Earnshaw equalised Pires' opener and Fábregas was again left to rue the team's lack of confidence. A couple of months ago, such a result would have been unthinkable. If Cesc and his colleagues did not recover soon, the Blues would be out of sight and the title would be heading to Stamford Bridge. It was hard to understand why things had gone downhill so quickly. It was not simply a case of the defence letting the team down – with the exception of the Tottenham game, the attackers were having problems too, and Arsenal were far from their free-scoring former selves.

Another miserable night awaited the Gunners in Eindhoven in midweek. The match ended 1-1, but Lauren and Vieira were sent off in the second half. Arsenal needed all of Fábregas' youthful energy to survive in the closing moments. It left Cesc and company needing to beat Rosenborg in their final group game to be certain of a place in the second round. Fábregas was left to wonder why the team always made life hard for themselves when it came to qualifying from the Champions League group stage. It should have been wrapped up by now.

Speaking to the media, Wenger tried to be positive in the wake of the draw in Holland: 'We defended well, and you are happy with a point when you have nine men. I am very confident we can still win the group and that's what we want to achieve.' With Vieira now suspended for the Rosenborg match, Cesc expected to be given extra responsibility in midfield. It would be nothing Fábregas could not handle and the Spaniard was determined that the prize of a place in the next round would not slip away.

A horrible November was finished off with a 2-1 defeat

at Anfield against Liverpool. More points dropped against their rivals angered the Gunners and Cesc knew that Mourinho was rubbing his hands with glee. With Campbell back in central defence and Fábregas lining up alongside Vieira, Arsenal looked strong on paper. But Liverpool outfought them as youngster Neil Mellor – getting his chance in the first team due to injuries – smashed a last-gasp winner from distance. It summed up the bad luck and below-par defending that had cost Cesc and company dearly since the defeat to United at Old Trafford. The players trudged off dejectedly yet again.

Wenger was far from impressed: 'Maybe we are suffering a little from fatigue and maybe our efforts with nine men in the Champions League have left us tired.' It was not one of Arsène's most convincing excuses and it did nothing to cover up the team's slump in form. Cesc and company just had to put the result behind them. The Spaniard also wanted to get into scoring positions more often to make himself a more complete midfielder and take the pressure off the strikers and wide players. Maybe this would help the side's goalscoring problems. One way or another, Arsenal had to start creating more chances.

The month of December breathed new life into the Gunners. Although Wenger's fledglings lost to Manchester United in the Carling Cup, the first-team regulars returned to top form as Arsenal put together a good run of results. A 3-0 win at home to Birmingham set the ball rolling. Fábregas was fortunate not to be punished for a poor back pass, but was otherwise his immaculate self, distributing the ball well and bringing Ljungberg, Pires and Henry into the game. Henry scored twice late on to give the scoreline a comfortable look.

A place in the Champions League second round was secured in midweek in emphatic fashion and other results even allowed Arsenal to top the group. A poor Rosenborg side were despatched 5-1 as the Gunners flexed their attacking muscles. Fábregas was one of the star men on the night, scoring the team's third goal with a fine half-volley after neat control. It put him in the record books yet again – this time as Arsenal's youngest ever goalscorer in Europe. Still just seventeen, it was incredible that Cesc could make his midfield role look so easy and the pundits were full of praise.

Wenger looked a relieved figure on the touchline, though he denied feeling the financial pressure of the Gunners' potential elimination. He told reporters: 'This was not a money evening for us; we could have survived being knocked out. What was at stake was our pride and ambition, as we want to be the best.'

Fábregas eagerly awaited the draw for the second round and looked forward to pitting his wits against another top side. The Spaniard got his wish: the Gunners were paired with German giants Bayern Munich – though he had a while to wait, as the Champions League took a break until the New Year.

It was the perfect preparation for Chelsea's visit to Highbury. On 12 December, the challengers and the champions squared in a match that received major hype from *Sky Sports*. Wenger and Mourinho would stand toe-to-toe and Fábregas would get another chance to ruffle the feathers of Frank Lampard, Claude Makelele and co. Cesc was involved early as he laid the ball forward and it eventually fell for Henry, who gave Arsenal the lead inside two minutes. The Blues had been caught cold. In the past, the Gunners would have powered on but, without Vieira and low on confidence, they allowed the Blues back into the game. Chelsea exploited the home side's newly-acquired inability to deal with set pieces as John Terry headed home an equaliser. Fábregas, not usually given the task of marking at corners, was frustrated to see the team concede again in that manner. More work was required on the training ground to put these lapses right.

A quickly taken free-kick from Henry restored Arsenal's advantage, but Mourinho tinkered with his formation at half-time and got instant results as Chelsea powered their way back into the game. Again it came from a set piece as Eidur Gudjohnsen looping the ball into the net. Both sides might have snatched a winner, but in the end had to settle for a 2-2 draw. As Cesc left the field, he knew the result did nothing to redress the balance in the title race. Arsenal had missed their chance to gain ground on the leaders, and the Blues left Highbury with even greater confidence in their ability to last the pace at the top.

Wenger revealed his disappointment post-match, but gave particular praise to Cesc and Mathieu Flamini, who formed a youthful midfield partnership: 'It's frustrating because we were twice in the lead, but we were pulled back. We had chances to win the game. In the middle of the park, our oldest player was twenty years old. I would like to congratulate the players for showing fantastic qualities.' Mourinho meanwhile claimed that Chelsea 'were the better team and should have won the game.'

The 2-2 draw may not have cut the Blues' lead, but it did remind the Arsenal squad that they were more than capable of matching Mourinho's side. Against Portsmouth at Fratton Park on 19 December, Fábregas was given a rest as Vieira returned to the midfield. A goal from Campbell was enough to earn a 1-0 victory and Arsène was able to keep Fábregas on the bench throughout, ensuring that the Spaniard had a proper break from the action. Missing the odd game allowed him to recharge his batteries and, along with the supplements Wenger had introduced at the club, it kept Cesc on track physically.

A week later, on Boxing Day, Wenger did not hesitate to bring Cesc back into the starting line-up for the home fixture against Fulham. Henry and Pires grabbed a goal each and the Gunners continued their promising December form. Fábregas looked fresher and passed the ball as crisply as ever. But it was back to the bench and a role as an unused substitute in the team's next match, a 1-0 win on Tyneside.

Back in the line-up away to Charlton, Fábregas strived to produce a performance that would make it impossible for Wenger to rest him again. The Spaniard's clever flick allowed Ljungberg to score the all-important second goal as the Gunners picked up another victory – 3-1 on this occasion.

But for some reason, the complacency and erratic performances returned to blight Arsenal over the next few weeks. A 1-1 draw at home to Manchester City was not good enough and Cesc knew it. He was substituted with the team trailing 1-0 and could only watch on as the Gunners grabbed an equaliser, and shared the disappointment when his team-mates failed to find a further breakthrough. Dropping two points here meant that Chelsea's lead at the top stretched to seven points. The momentum was undoubtedly with the Blues. A 2-1 win over Stoke saw Fábregas and a youthful Arsenal side begin their FA Cup campaign in positive fashion. With any dreams of the Premiership title slipping from their grasp, Fábregas and his team-mates were looking to other competitions for a more realistic chance of silverware.

Bolton once more proved to be the Gunners' bogey team. Sam Allardyce seemed to have discovered the right approach against Wenger's passing style and the Trotters frustrated Arsenal for long periods. Stelios Giannakopoulos scored the first-half winner as Fábregas and company drew a blank – a rarity for such an attacking side. Cesc played just over an hour of the contest before making way for compatriot Reyes. The defeat put a massive dent in the Gunners' title bid – Chelsea were lengthening the gap week by week.

With a pivotal clash against Manchester United ahead, Fábregas and his team-mates were desperate to build up some momentum before facing Ferguson's side. The Spaniard was eager to gain revenge for the 2-0 loss earlier in the season; one that had ended Arsenal's unbeaten run and sent the club into temporary freefall. A 1-0 victory over Newcastle brought a welcome clean sheet, though Cesc remained an unused substitute for the game. The three points won saw the Gunners move back into second place, but the entire squad knew it would take something special to claw back the ten-point gap between themselves and Jose Mourinho's Chelsea.

An FA Cup fourth-round tie with Wolves brought back fond memories for Fábregas. The youngster had opened his goalscoring account for Arsenal against Wolves in the previous season's Carling Cup. Sadly, though, there would be no repeat. The Gunners won 2-0, but Cesc only came off the bench for the final fifteen minutes.

If he had been disappointed to be left out of the line-up to face Wolves, one can only imagine his agony at being named as a substitute for the clash with United. Fábregas had been desperate to play in such a huge contest, but perhaps Wenger felt that Cesc's temperament was not ready for the type of heated clash it promised to be at Highbury. Maybe it was the correct decision. It was no secret the two sets of players did not like each other, but nobody could have predicted that the animosity would start in the tunnel – before the match even kicked off!

Patrick Vieira and Roy Keane, the two captains, were involved in a simmering argument over something the Arsenal skipper had allegedly said to United defender Gary Neville as the teams headed to the changing rooms after the warm-up. It ensured the game itself would be feisty, as both teams looked fired up by the fracas. Cesc took his place on the Gunners bench and tried not to feel too aggrieved. He was soon celebrating, though, as Vieira put Arsenal ahead. Ryan Giggs equalised for United ten minutes later as the match swung from end to end and tempers came to the boil. Wayne Rooney was fortunate to stay on the pitch after several clattering challenges and a mouthful of abuse directed at the referee. To Cesc's delight, Highbury was rocking again when Dennis Bergkamp pounced to send the Gunners in at half-time with a 2-1 lead.

But after the interval, Fábregas watched his worst nightmare unfold before his eyes as United took control. Keane began to dominate midfield and his team-mates responded. Cristiano Ronaldo fired home an equaliser and, with the Gunners looking shell-shocked, the Portuguese winger scored again four minutes later from Giggs' cross. Mikael Silvestre was sent off with twenty minutes remaining and Arsenal pushed forward in search of a way back into the game. Cesc was finally brought on in the last ten minutes, but by then the Gunners had become desperate, resorting to a more direct style of play. In the end, it was United who found the knockout blow as John O'Shea placed an exquisite chip over Almunia to seal a 4-2 win for the visitors.

Highbury was silent and the Arsenal players trudged off, knowing they could forget about their title dreams. They had played poorly in the second half and could have no complaints. Fábregas was doubly disappointed. He was saddened by the result, but also by the fact that he had only been given seven minutes to shine. Maybe he could have influenced the scoreline if he had been on the pitch for longer. However, there would be plenty more clashes with United for him to look forward to.

Before the match, Wenger had admitted that whoever lost this fixture would be out of the title race and, true to his word, he told the media that the Premiership trophy was now out of reach for Arsenal: 'We will not give up, but now we are too far behind. It's Chelsea's title now. United still have a slight chance, but there is too much for us to do.' It was only the beginning of February. Suddenly, the FA Cup and Champions League took on an even greater significance for Cesc and his team-mates. Their league campaign had gone off the rails.

There was no point in feeling sorry for themselves. They simply had to get on with the job and the Gunners did just that away to Aston Villa. Fábregas was again left on the bench until the final ten minutes, but would have been relieved to see his colleagues put the game to bed with three goals in the first half hour. With Edu and Vieira performing well in the centre of midfield, Cesc had to be patient and wait for his chance. It would be a difficult spell for the Spaniard because, having featured so regularly earlier in the campaign, a substitute's role was one he would have to get used to in the coming weeks. And things were complicated by the fact Cesc had to deal with reports about his parents getting a divorce. It was all pretty upsetting and at the time left him shaken.

A 5-1 victory over Crystal Palace at Highbury saw Fábregas used as a late substitute once again. The fixture went down in the history books as the first time a side had ever selected a 16-man squad for a Premiership game that did not contain a single Englishman. The media focused in on this fact and questioned Wenger's policy over home-grown players.

Fábregas was back in the starting line-up for Arsenal's FA Cup-tie against Sheffield United at Highbury. It was a below-par Arsenal performance and a late penalty earned the visitors a replay at Bramall Lane. For Cesc, it had not been the return he was hoping for, although he offered occasional glimpses of his talent and forced a good save from United goalkeeper Paddy Kenny. With Champions League commitments ahead, Fábregas knew the Gunners' schedule could have done without an FA Cup replay.

The fact Cesc was in contention for a starting place again was an exceptional achievement. Despite his inexperience, he had given Wenger, who was trying to keep all of his midfielders happy, a big selection headache. In midweek, the Gunners travelled to Germany for the Champions League second-round first leg against Bayern Munich. With so much now riding on their European form, there was plenty of pressure on the team to perform. Fábregas was named in the squad, but once again had to settle for a place among the substitutes.

And that was where he stayed all night. From that vantage point, he had an up-close view of a shambolic Arsenal display that put the Gunners on the brink of elimination from the competition. Defensive wobbles again hurt the team as Bayern exploited a back four missing Campbell and Ashley Cole. The normally reliable Kolo Toure had a night to forget. The Germans took an early lead, but the score remained 1-0 at half-time and some felt as though Arsenal had weathered the storm. Fábregas was optimistic that an away goal in the second half could pull the side back into the contest. But it was Bayern who seized the initiative, scoring twice in seven minutes. Though Toure grabbed a late goal for the Gunners, Cesc knew that a 3-1 defeat would be hard to overturn at home.

It had been a cold and frustrating night for the Spaniard. Watching his team-mates crumble on a chilly night in Munich, Fábregas was left downbeat. An injury to Edu before half-time had forced a substitution, but Wenger had opted to send on Flamini rather than Cesc. The youngster had done little wrong during the season and was disappointed to see his first-team appearances suddenly limited.

Wenger may not have been irate after the match, but he found it hard to hide his disappointment with the display:

'The players are really down in the dressing room. I feel we really turned in a bad performance.' There was little laughter on the flight home as Cesc and his colleagues digested the painful loss. Even though the Spaniard had taken no part in the action, he was learning all the time from being around the team on such occasions and from watching the action intently. He might not have realised it at the time, but it was a vital part of his football education. Wenger was keen to make sure the youngster was aware of the different systems European teams employed and of the need to show extra patience in the Champions League.

Fábregas did not feature at St Mary's in a 1-1 draw with Southampton, but returned to action at Sheffield United for the FA Cup replay. He was certainly fresh, and his performance showed it. His energetic runs stretched the United midfield and he went close to scoring on several occasions; his finishing needed to be a fraction better. The game headed into extra-time, but the Spaniard was replaced by Toure for the additional thirty minutes. The game remained goalless and Cesc had to watch nervously as the Gunners prevailed on penalties to keep the FA Cup run alive.

On 5 March, a morale-boosting win at home to Portsmouth gave the team some much-needed confidence ahead of the return match with Bayern. Fábregas was again in the side and played well. Henry took all the headlines, though, as he bagged a hat-trick. But had Cesc done enough to earn a starting berth against the Germans?

The answer, sadly for the Spaniard, was no. Wenger paired Vieira with Flamini and kept Fábregas among the substitutes for the big night at Highbury. It would take a special performance to topple Bayern, but not an unthinkable one – after all, a 2-0 victory would suffice. The Germans, however, were typically well-organised and presented the Gunners with few openings. In fact, the visitors went closer themselves. With over an hour gone, Arsène sent Cesc into the fray and the substitution bore fruit immediately. Lifted by the creativity of Fábregas and fellow replacement Pires, Arsenal took the lead on the night through Henry. It made it 3-2 on aggregate to Bayern, but one more goal for the Gunners would put them through on away goals.

Hard though they tried, Cesc and his team-mates could not find that elusive goal. The game ended 1-0 and Arsenal were out. They had come so close to rescuing the disastrous night in Munich and this must have made elimination even harder to take. Should Wenger have been bolder and picked the Spaniard from the start at Highbury? It was a valid question and one that cropped up in plenty of post-match debates. Cesc might have made the difference on a night when Arsenal found it tough to get into their usual, fluent rhythm.

Next Arsenal shifted their focus to the FA Cup, the only trophy left to play for, and they had been drawn against Bolton of all teams! On this occasion, though, Arsenal stayed strong. They were helped by an early goal and then El-Hadji Diouf's foolish red card for elbowing Lehmann. Fábregas was an unused substitute, but was relieved that the dream of making it to the Millennium Stadium was becoming a real possibility. Though Cesc was always eager to play, Wenger deserved great credit for holding him back and introducing the seventeen-year-old slowly to the strain of first-team football.

Fábregas played the full ninety minutes at Blackburn on 19 March as Arsenal kept up their pursuit of second spot – it would be a big plus if the Gunners did not have to play qualifiers to earn their Champions League place and it would allow the squad to enjoy a longer summer break. Van Persie scored the winner after a delightful build-up involving Cesc and then Cole. Fábregas was everywhere, tackling back one minute; shooting for goal the next. Once again he was showing Wenger that he could handle the pressure of English football. It was a good win against a stubborn Rovers side.

Two more Premiership wins kept the Gunners on course for second place. A 4-1 win over Norwich at Highbury was emphatic and reminded everyone of the gulf that existed between the top sides and the league minnows. An injury to Flamini saw Fábregas brought on before half-time with Arsenal already 2-0 up. The second half saw the Gunners cruise to victory. A week later, Cesc put in another good display away to Middlesbrough and was part of the move that led to the Arsenal's winner in a 1-0 triumph. The team's form since losing to Manchester United had been excellent.

The importance of the FA Cup semi-final against Blackburn on 16 April was not lost on Fábregas. The competition represented the Gunners' final chance to salvage something from their season – just as had been the case for Manchester United the previous year when they faced Arsenal at the same stage of the competition. Just twelve months on from the Invincibles campaign, Cesc could not contemplate the possibility of a trophy-less season. As one of the new additions to the side, he feared attention might unfairly be drawn to the team's downward slide since his introduction to the first team.

The clash with Blackburn proved a typically physical contest. As one would expect from a team containing the likes of Lucas Neill, Andy Todd and Paul Dickov, Rovers were not shy to throw themselves into challenges. Fábregas began among the substitutes, but joined the action just after half-time, replacing Ljungberg.

Pires had put Arsenal ahead after forty-two minutes, but the match remained tight as Cesc and company failed to make the most of their chances. Fábregas himself was guilty of a couple of misses but, just as importantly, he kept his cool in the heated atmosphere. Van Persie secured the team's place in the final with two goals in the last four minutes as Blackburn pushed for an equaliser.

After the Dutchman's second strike, he collided with Todd's elbow in a nasty incident that incensed Wenger and the Arsenal players, who felt that the defender may have made contact deliberately. Arsène raged at the post-match press conference about the general aggression shown by Rovers: 'We responded to some over-the-edge fouls, but kept great focus on the game and never lost our nerve. For a young team that was remarkable. I don't feel that Andy Todd needed to lift his elbow. He could have stopped himself.'

On a more positive note, Cesc was delighted to be heading to the FA Cup final – his first final as an Arsenal player. It was a competition he had long admired and now the Gunners would be appearing in the showpiece finale. Their opponents would be Manchester United, who comfortably beat Newcastle in the other semi-final. If the two league meetings between the two sides that season were any indication, it promised to be an enthralling contest.

While Chelsea sat a whole eleven points clear of Arsenal in the Premiership table, Fábregas was hopeful that he and his team-mates could finish above Manchester United to clinch second place. The Gunners missed a late chance to close the gap on the leaders as they drew 0-0 with Mourinho's side at Stamford Bridge on 20 April. Cesc was selected in midfield and stood his ground against more experienced opponents and it was a good sign that Arsenal were able to emerge with a point against the soon-to-be champions.

The Gunners' consistency was impressing everyone – it was just a shame that they had left their surge so late. A 1-0 victory over Tottenham in the second North London derby of the season gave the Arsenal fans plenty to cheer about, with Reyes grabbing the winner after receiving an inch-perfect pass from Fábregas. Cesc's vision had unlocked a stubborn Spurs defence and his team-mates crowded round him to show their appreciation. This was the type of moment he had in mind when he said that for him creating a goal was preferable to scoring one. It gave him great satisfaction to have engineered this key moment.

A 2-0 win at West Brom on 2 May was followed by a super 3-1 triumph over Liverpool at Highbury in a memorable match for Fábregas. The Spaniard set up the team's second goal for Reyes and then sealed the victory by scoring the third himself, finishing a typically fluent Arsenal attack after Bergkamp's assist. Gaining three points against Liverpool was no mean feat. While it condemned Rafa Benitez's side to fifth place in the table

– behind local rivals Everton – the Merseyside club would go on to win the Champions League later that month in dramatic fashion against Italian giants AC Milan. Trailing 3-0 at half-time, Liverpool fought back to draw 3-3 and win on penalties.

Things got even better for the Gunners in midweek as they turned on the style against Everton. Cesc began on the bench, but came on for almost half an hour to drive the side forward towards a 7-0 win. Almost as remarkably, there were six different scorers. It was vintage Arsenal and Fábregas was especially proud to be part of the squad that night. Bergkamp, one of the scorers, had not yet agreed a new deal at the club and so there was the possibility that this had been his final league appearance at Highbury. It was an emotional ninety minutes. Everton were set to finish fourth in the table yet they had been blown away by the Gunners.

Though there was still one more Premiership fixture remaining, all the Arsenal players began to cast their minds towards the FA Cup final. Cesc was by no means certain of making the starting line-up, but he hoped his recent displays had put him in contention. It would be a sensational feeling to walk out onto the field on such a massive occasion. Before that, though, the Gunners faced Birmingham in their final league match of the season. But Fábregas and company produced a far from convincing performance as the team appeared to be going through the motions, hoping not to get injured before the cup final. Arsenal lost 2-1, but nonetheless finished in second place, ensuring automatic qualification for the following season's Champions League.

There was just the small matter of an FA Cup final left

for Cesc to look forward to. He could not wait to sample the atmosphere inside the Millennium Stadium. Manchester United would undoubtedly be tough opponents as both teams were relying on the FA Cup to rescue their campaign. Ferguson's side had won both the league matches during the season and revenge was definitely on the menu for Fábregas and his team-mates, no matter what they said publicly. The manner of their defeat at Old Trafford earlier in the campaign had not been erased from the players' memories and it gave Cesc all the motivation he needed.

The bad news for Arsenal came in the form of Henry's enforced absence due to injury. It caused Wenger to rethink his tactics and decide on a more defensive 4-5-1 formation, leaving Bergkamp up front on his own. Cesc received the verdict that he had been praying for. He was in the starting line-up, playing alongside Vieira and Gilberto in central midfield. It was a rather negative approach from the Gunners, but the Spaniard agreed with Wenger – the team would do whatever it took to lift the cup.

The walk out onto the pitch at the Millennium Stadium was something Fábregas would never forget – the excitement, the nerves, the emotions. He was so proud to be representing Arsenal in the FA Cup final. With both teams using the same formation, a predictable stalemate ensued. Rooney and Ronaldo caused major problems for the Gunners' full-backs and Cesc found himself spending a lot of time chasing back and helping the defence. There was so little space in the central midfield areas and the Spaniard found it tough to get into his usual rhythm. Arsenal created little going forward and were grateful to

Lehmann for keeping them in the contest with several good saves.

A frustrating afternoon ended for Fábregas after eighty-six minutes when Wenger took him off and brought on van Persie. Cesc had worked diligently for the cause, but it was not the type of flowing match he enjoyed. He took his place in the stands and cheered on his colleagues. Arsenal seemed to decide that a penalty shootout was their best chance of victory and played even more negatively during extra-time – a period that saw Reyes red-carded in the final moments. When the final whistle blew, 120 minutes of football had been unable to separate the two teams and the cup would be decided by spot-kicks for the first time in its history.

Fábregas, who might well have put his name forward for penalty-taking responsibilities, sat glued to the action. Lehmann proved to be the hero that afternoon in Cardiff as he made the decisive save, pushing aside Scholes' penalty. Vieira netted the winning kick and the Arsenal celebrations began. Cesc had won his first medal at the club. It was an incredible feeling as he joined in the lap of honour and he could not wait to get his hands on the famous trophy. The side's supporters stayed on after the final whistle to join in with the party and Fábregas felt the buzz of winning his first major club honour.

Wenger was delighted with the team's character, even if the normal attacking style was missing from the display: 'We really had to dig deep. I'm very proud because it was a difficult game. There were some times in the second half when we were a bit lucky, but we defended very well and to keep a clean sheet is good.' Ferguson, meanwhile, drew attention to the referee's leniency towards Vieira and Reyes, who the United boss felt should have been sent off earlier.

For Fábregas, it was undoubtedly one of the most exciting days of his life. He knew he had not played to his potential, but it had been a tricky game for a youngster and he had given his all. In general, though, the season had not been a success for the Gunners and winning the FA Cup did not change the fact that the team had been erratic for large chunks of the campaign. Cesc, Wenger and the rest of the set-up were well aware that the Premiership and the Champions League were the competitions that mattered most, and Arsenal had fallen short in both. Though a repeat of the unbeaten league run was never a realistic target, Cesc and his team-mates had expected to be challenging for top honours again. Sadly, since late October, they had never looked like doing so.

Fábregas' breakthrough season was not over yet though. Selected as part of the Spanish squad for the Under-20 World Cup, the youngster headed off to Holland for the tournament. In truth, the long, arduous campaign in England left Cesc a little below par, but he was determined to put on a good show for the Spanish supporters. The team were drawn in Group C alongside Morocco, Chile and Honduras. Having performed so well at the Under-17 competition in Finland in 2003, Spain were among the favourites to add the Under-20 World Cup to their trophy cabinet, but the likes of Argentina and Brazil would doubtless run them close.

The competition began for the Spanish on 11 June against the Moroccans. A solid team display clinched a 3-1 victory and Cesc played the full ninety minutes. The side were living up to their top billing and a 7-0 demolition of Chile three days later showed that Spain meant serious business. Leading just 1-0 at the interval, Fábregas and his team-mates ran riot in the second half against a Chile side who had beaten Honduras 7-0 in their first fixture. Spanish striker Fernando Llorente scored four as Cesc enjoyed one of his easiest matches of the year. Again he played the full game, despite the team's dominance.

Spain completed a flawless group stage by beating Honduras 3-0 in their final Group C fixture. Fábregas was given the chance to rest during the first half, but came off the bench for the second period. Nine points out of a possible nine represented a great start and the team now looked forward to their second-round game. Their opponents would be Turkey, who had been erratic in their Group A displays.

The Turks were no match for the Spaniards on 22 June as they completed a routine 3-0 victory. With the game wrapped up, Cesc was substituted with thirty minutes remaining in order to keep him fresh. He was such a big star and the management wanted him to be full of running for future rounds. The quarter-finals pitted Fábregas' Spain side against Lionel Messi's Argentina – a fixture that should really have been a semi-final or final. But the Argentines had finished second in their group and were forced to take a tougher route.

It was a big match for Cesc and his team-mates, but they could not find the form that had swept them through the group stage. Argentina were too strong on the day and it was Messi himself who sealed victory for his team, scoring the third in a 3-1 win. It was a frustrating match for Fábregas, but he could not argue with the outcome – Argentina had been worthy winners. Spain had beaten them narrowly in the 2003 semi-final, but this time Messi had had the last laugh. The Argentines went on to lift the trophy, triumphing over Nigeria in the final.

Having set out to go all the way to the final of the tournament, defeat came as a big blow for the Spaniards. Most people had expected them to reach the last four. Cesc had not been prolific in front of goal and was unable to produce the kinds of performances that had lit up the Under-17 World Cup in 2003. But he was not coming into the tournament feeling as fresh as many of the other players. He had done his best, but he was well aware that Spain had underachieved.

He had World Cups under his belt now at Under-17 and Under-20 level, so the next natural step for the young midfield star was to feature for the senior squad at a major tournament. The 2006 World Cup was fast approaching, but Euro 2008 looked like the more realistic target, if Cesc could maintain his exciting form. His talent was reaching wider audiences and his reputation was growing, yet he appeared capable of taking it all in his stride. He was quickly becoming accustomed to handling the spotlight.

As the Spaniard headed off for a few weeks of rest, he hoped his performances during the long campaign had impressed spectators and that he would have an even bigger role to play when the new Premiership season kicked off in August.

CHAPTER 3

THE EUROPEAN ADVENTURE

As the new season arrived, Fábregas was eager to build on his promising first full campaign for the Gunners. He had received rave reviews from the media and would be thrust further into the spotlight after the summer dealings at Highbury. Wenger accepted a bid from Juventus for Patrick Vieira and the French midfielder headed to Italy in a £13.75 million move. It sent shockwaves of panic around the club but, for Cesc, it had opened the door even further. In the absence of Vieira, he would undoubtedly see more first-team minutes.

Fábregas had learned a huge amount from the now-former Gunners skipper during their time together at Arsenal and will always be thankful for the advice and encouragement he received. He had been able to talk things over with Vieira on countless occasions and it had undoubtedly improved his understanding of the game. It was a shame the duo had not been able to play in midfield together for more years. Cesc was saddened to hear of Vieira's exit, but he was excited by the prospect of filling the Frenchman's boots.

Wenger obviously had no doubts over Fábregas' ability to play a full season in central midfield. Many speculated about which big-name star Arsène would sign to replace Vieira, but the Gunners boss knew he had no need to dabble in the transfer market – he already had the ideal candidate in his squad. It was a huge boost for Cesc and he looked forward to the new campaign more eagerly than ever. All eyes would be on him.

As Fábregas explained in a more recent magazine interview, he was eager to repay the faith Wenger had shown in him. Recalling the 2005/06 season, Cesc said: 'I knew it was a big chance for me to show everyone that the boss was not wrong and that I could be there to replace him [Vieira].' The Spaniard also heaped praise on his manager's instincts over youngsters: 'He is not scared of giving opportunities. That's why I'm so thankful to Arsène Wenger.'

Cesc was becoming a more central figure in English football. In an interview with *CBBC Newsround*, the midfielder discussed his rise at Arsenal. Young fans all over the country wrote in with questions. What advice did he have for young hopefuls? 'If you are eight or ten, then just enjoy it. You are only a child and you should just play with your friends. When they are fifteen, work hard as there might be chances to take.' Does he miss Spain? 'To be honest, I'm really, really happy in London. It's a great city with great people and I'm not thinking about missing Spain as I am so busy and don't have much spare time.' Fábregas always enjoyed interacting with the young Gunners fans because, as he recalled from his own childhood, 'I would have loved to have the chance to talk to the players who were my idols when I was younger.'

Elsewhere in the Premiership, Arsenal's rivals were very active in the transfer market. Unsurprisingly, Chelsea again flexed their financial muscles as Mourinho added midfielders Michael Essien and Shaun Wright-Phillips and left-back Asier Del Horno to an already impressive squad. The three new faces cost in excess of £50 million. Manchester United, meanwhile, were quieter over the summer and just added goalkeeper Edwin van der Sar from Fulham and South Korean Ji-Sung Park. United fans had been rocked by the news that Malcolm Glazer had bought the club and there were huge protests over this issue. Liverpool, the European champions, made several signings, including 6ft 7in front man Peter Crouch, but still did not appear capable of winning the league. Benitez's side were lacking that little bit of extra quality needed to last the pace.

Having finished second last season, the Gunners were pleased to have avoided the Champions League qualifiers. Instead, they completed a stress-free pre-season and focused on their first league game – at home to Newcastle. Cesc lined up alongside Gilberto in the centre of midfield and life became much easier after Jermaine Jenas was sent off in the thirty-second minute; now there was more space for Fábregas to set up crisp passing moves but the goals would not come. Wenger substituted Cesc with just under twenty minutes to go and the youngster watched nervously as his team-mates laid siege to the Newcastle goal. He joined in the celebrations as Henry finally broke the deadlock from the penalty spot and van Persie made sure of the points minutes later.

Fábregas knew the Gunners would see plenty more sides coming to Highbury with the same mentality as Newcastle – playing one man up front, five in midfield and defending in numbers. Cesc found this negative approach particularly frustrating and against all his football principles. His education at Barcelona, and indeed at Arsenal, had taught him to play in a positive, creative manner. To him, football was about entertainment as well as winning. Why would teams deliberately set out to defend in numbers and never look to push men forward? It was something he would have to learn to cope with, because Arsenal would need plenty of his precise passes to unlock stubborn defences over the course of the season. It would require character and patience if visiting teams were going to be overcome.

Next for the Gunners was a tough assignment away to the champions, Chelsea. Jose Mourinho's side had had the better of Arsenal the previous season and Fábregas was eager to prove things would be different in 2005/06. But it was the Blues who had the last laugh, winning 1-0 thanks to a Didier Drogba goal. Cesc's good friend, Phillipe Senderos, made the crucial mistake to present Drogba with his chance. Fábregas toiled for eighty-five minutes in midfield, but Chelsea were too strong. It was a frustrating afternoon for the Spaniard. Mourinho's side appeared to be stronger than ever and intent on setting the pace at the top. There were no signs of complacency at Stamford Bridge.

The next few weeks brought more erratic form for the Gunners and questions were asked of Wenger's decision to sell Vieira. Arsenal could be brilliant one week and then feeble the next and it was having a damaging effect on their title chances. At home to Fulham on 24 August, Arsenal had one of their good days, winning 4-1 with defender Pascal Cygan and Thierry Henry grabbing two goals each. For the latter, the brace moved him one behind Ian Wright's club goalscoring record. Fábregas almost gave his side the lead early on and he played the full ninety minutes for the first time that season.

But the Gunners went from sublime to ridiculous two weeks later. Wenger opted to leave Cesc on the bench for the trip to Middlesbrough and the Spaniard could only watch on as his team-mates surrendered in feeble fashion to the home side. Arsenal had a host of chances, failed to take them and then conceded goals to Yakubu and Massimo Maccarone. After Maccarone put Boro 2-0 up, Fábregas was sent on to try to rescue something from the match. Reyes scored in the final moments, but it was too little too late. The discussion over the departure of Vieira rumbled on – the Gunners were looking worryingly lightweight without the powerful Frenchman.

The start of the Champions League schedule came as a welcome distraction. Arsenal had been drawn in Group B along with FC Thun of Switzerland, Sparta Prague of the Czech Republic and the well-known Dutch side, Ajax. The campaign began at home to FC Thun and the three points should have been a formality. Fábregas was back in the starting line-up, but the Gunners still struggled to make a breakthrough. Gilberto eventually opened the scoring after half-time, only for FC Thun to equalise within two minutes. Bergkamp replaced Cesc and the Dutchman finally settled the contest in the final seconds. It should not have been this difficult and Fábregas knew the team needed to be more clinical. A 2-0 victory at home to Everton on 19 September was much more comfortable, with Sol Campbell bagging both goals.

A 0-0 draw away to West Ham, though, brought more frustration. With Henry injured, the team was struggling to find the net and Fábregas did not help matters by wasting one glorious opportunity. The Hammers had a couple of late chances and in the end Arsenal had to settle for a point. Cesc was well aware that the Gunners were slipping behind the leaders and needed to be more consistent. If standards did not improve, they could forget about the title. Again, they were making life easy for Chelsea rather than putting the Blues under pressure.

Arsenal's away form in Europe had often let them down, so Fábregas was delighted when he and his team-mates recorded a 2-1 victory away to Ajax on 27 September. Goals from Ljungberg and Pires – from the penalty spot – ensured that the flight back from Amsterdam was a happy one. Six points out of six was an excellent start and the Gunners seemed on course for the second round. The previous season's early elimination at the hands of Bayern Munich still haunted Cesc and company and they were determined to progress further this time around. The squad were keen to move into the bracket of world-class teams and to do so they needed to lift the Champions League trophy. Having watched his beloved Barcelona triumph in Europe in 1992, Cesc understood what all the fuss was about.

A 1-0 win over Birmingham kept up the momentum, but a 2-1 defeat at West Brom on 15 October provided Fábregas and his team-mates with another disappointing away day. Senderos had put Arsenal ahead, but they surrendered meekly. Cesc thought he had found the net with a fine strike, only to see goalkeeper Chris Kirkland make a brilliant save. The Spaniard worked hard throughout the match, but Gunners fans were yet to be convinced that the new-look midfield could match the standards set by Vieira. Opposition sides were suddenly less intimidated when they faced Arsenal, knowing they were less likely to be overpowered in the centre of the field.

But the setback at the Hawthorns stirred the Gunners into life and, with Fábregas to the fore, went on an unbeaten run in all competitions that stretched into December. It began in the Czech Republic as Sparta Prague were beaten 2-0 with Henry scoring both goals after coming on as an early substitute. Cesc was enjoying the flowing football the side were playing and knew he had numerous outlets when in possession, with Pires and Henry in particularly good form.

That same duo had a less impressive moment in the team's next game against Manchester City at Highbury. Pires had already put the Gunners ahead from the penalty spot when referee Mike Riley awarded Arsenal another spot-kick. The two Frenchmen chose this moment to try out a routine pioneered by Ajax duo Johann Cruyff and Jesper Olsen in which the penalty taker runs up, taps the ball forward and a team-mate runs from the edge of the box to slot the ball home. However, Pires made a mess of his role and the plan was ruined. Fábregas was just relieved that the side held on for the 1-0 win and three points – Wenger would have had plenty to say if City had equalised late on. Instead, Cesc was able to enjoy the banter in the dressing room after the game. It was safe to say the routine would not be tested again any time soon.

With his status as a first-team player secured, Fábregas was rested from the Carling Cup-tie with Sunderland. Although he was always eager to play, Wenger had to be firm with the youngster, telling him that he needed a break to avoid burnout. Arsenal advanced to the next round with a 3-0 win and momentum started to build up around the club. It seemed like only yesterday that the Spaniard was taking his bow in the competition – he had come a very long way since then.

However, the Gunners failed to show much of their improved form at White Hart Lane in the North London derby on 29 October. Tottenham led at half-time and Fábregas and his team-mates needed an error from Spurs goalkeeper Paul Robinson to snatch an equaliser with less than fifteen minutes remaining. Cesc felt disappointed to have let the Arsenal fans down with the below-par first-half performance and he was annoyed that he had struggled to break the shackles of the Tottenham midfield. Although North London derbies are always tricky affairs, Fábregas viewed the result as two points dropped, especially as Chelsea had already amassed a strong lead at the top of the table.

Nonetheless, Cesc was performing well and could not be blamed for the team's indifferent form. He had been thrown in at the deep end and had adjusted superbly, especially considering he was still just eighteen years of age. It was a tough ask for Fábregas to step into a team with so many respected figures and play with confidence. As a result, he sometimes deferred to his more illustrious team-mates at times when he could have delivered the key pass or taken the shot himself. But when Bergkamp or Henry called for the ball, it was only natural that Cesc felt inclined to find them. In time, this tendency would disappear.

Fábregas came off the bench in midweek as Arsenal continued to dominate their Champions League group. The Gunners secured a 3-0 win over Sparta Prague and took their place in the second round of the competition. Four wins out of four was an excellent record. With the score at 1-0, Cesc came on and played the final twenty minutes as the team extended their advantage thanks to two van Persie goals. Qualification had been achieved so comfortably that Arsène Wenger could now rest some of his first-team players for the final two group games.

Wenger restored Fábregas to the starting line-up for Sunderland's visit to Highbury. The Black Cats had no answer to the Gunners' slick passing as Arsenal took a 2-0 lead before half-time. Sunderland pulled a goal back and might have been thinking about sneaking a point when Cesc took centre stage. He collected possession and played the perfect through ball for Henry to settle the contest. In such moments, the Spaniard looked like a seasoned veteran out on the pitch and Arsène hoped for more of the same.

A trip to Wigan on 19 November saw Fábregas again in the thick of the action. The Gunners picked up a well-earned 3-2 win, but could have won by more. Cesc was among those who missed decent opportunities and his bust-up with Wigan striker Jason Roberts led to pushing and shoving involving both sets of players. Fábregas was determined to show he was no pushover, but perhaps he had let his temper get the better of him on this occasion. It was something he would have to be careful about.

Cesc was left on the bench for the meaningless Champions League tie with FC Thun as Wenger once again took the opportunity to keep him fresh. The Spaniard had already clocked up a lot of minutes over the first four months of the season and the Arsenal manager was cautious about asking too much of him. Not that Cesc would have complained. He hated missing out on any match – important or not. With the game still goalless, Wenger sent Cesc on before the hour mark. The Gunners had to wait until the eighty-eighth minute before making the breakthrough as Pires scored from the spot to make it five wins out of five for the men from Highbury.

The following weekend, Cesc went toe-to-toe with a physical Blackburn midfield and showed his progress by coming out on top. The Gunners recorded a 3-0 victory and Fábregas played a key role, scoring the opening goal with a well-placed shot. It was fitting that, on the day that the football world mourned the death of the legendary George Best, Cesc – together with Henry – put on a masterclass worthy of the great man. Best had been an incredible player, it was an emotional day all over Britain and Fábregas had produced a performance befitting the occasion. Performances like this made it inevitable that a place in the Spanish senior squad would soon be coming his way.

After Arsenal's Carling Cup side had disposed of Championship leaders Reading, the first-team players saw their good run come to end against their nemesis Bolton. Two first-half goals for the Trotters put the game beyond the Gunners and Fábregas was substituted with around twenty minutes left. It had been a difficult afternoon for him as Bolton denied him time and space and made good use of the long ball, unsettling the Arsenal defence. A forgettable few weeks followed, and the wear and tear of the season began to show on the young Spanish star.

Fábregas made a half-hour cameo against Ajax in the Champions League on 7 December. The match finished 0-0, but mattered little as the Gunners were already thinking about the next round. Far more worrying was a 1-0 defeat at St James' Park in which Arsenal laboured against committed opponents who worked hard in packs to frustrate Cesc and his team-mates. Gilberto was shown a red card before the hour mark for a second bookable offence and it left the side a little rattled in midfield. Fábregas was constantly harried by a handful of eager Newcastle defenders and found his influence restricted. Consequently, the Gunners never got going. Nolberto Solano popped up with a late winner and the media again questioned Wenger's decision to sell Vieira.

Fábregas' hopes of competing for the title seemed to have disappeared. Chelsea were in unstoppable form. There was a resiliency about their team that had not been so evident under former boss Claudio Ranieri. This is where Arsenal had fallen down. As had been the case the previous season, Mourinho's side had mastered the art of consistency and managed to grind out victories even when not at their best. John Terry and Frank Lampard had flourished under Mourinho's management. On form, the Gunners were unstoppable, but when they struggled, points invariably were dropped.

A chance for Wenger's team to redeem themselves was just around the corner, though: Chelsea were the next visitors to Highbury on 18 December. While a victory was unlikely to revive Arsenal's title bid, Fábregas was desperate to prove a point to the Blues and restore some pride to the club. Unfortunately, the Gunners' woes continued as Mourinho's side strolled into North London and thoroughly deserved their 2-0 win. The game was fiery but, when the dust settled, it was Terry, Lampard and company who could celebrate a significant victory.

It was more than Fábregas could bear and the Premiership table made horrific viewing for Gunners fans. Chelsea were twenty points ahead of Arsenal, who had one game in hand. The media wasted no time in mentioning the fact that not long ago Wenger's side had been dubbed the 'Invincibles' – now that tag looked utterly out of place. It was Mourinho's team that deserved that moniker – they were sweeping all before them domestically for the second season in a row and Cesc could have no complaints about the quality and commitment of the Blues' displays.

Arsène was angry after the game, rightly claiming that a van Persie 'goal' had been wrongly disallowed, but in reality he could have very few complaints about the scoreline. The Gunners had been outclassed. Fábregas could forget about chasing the title. More important was their bid to claim a Champions League spot – and, given the extent of the Gunners' struggles, even this was looking in doubt. Worst of all for the club was the progress Tottenham were making. The Arsenal supporters would never live it down if their North London rivals pipped them to a Champions League place.

Cesc had to re-evaluate his aims for the season. While the Premiership had slipped away again, there was still plenty left to play for. The youngsters progressed in the Carling Cup and the first-team stars seemed to feed off their spirit, picking up two important victories over the Christmas period. A goal from Reyes was enough to see off Charlton at The Valley on Boxing Day and Fábregas breathed a sigh of relief – the team were back to winning ways. But they had a lot of work ahead of them if they wanted to reel in the leaders.

A 4-0 win over Portsmouth on 28 December saw the Gunners finally take out their frustrations from a rough month. Fábregas was rested for the fixture and had a perfect view of the demolition from the touchline. All four goals came in the first half and so the game was over as a contest by the time Fábregas replaced Gilberto in the second period. He was disappointed not to have featured earlier in the match, but was delighted with the way his team-mates had performed. Most felt that Wenger was doing a good job of regulating the youngster's minutes – it would benefit nobody if Cesc suffered a fatigue-related injury. Arsène was thinking of the future.

Fábregas returned to face Aston Villa, but could not conjure the all-important goal as the Gunners lost more ground on the top sides, drawing 0-0 in the Midlands. Tottenham and Bolton looked set to fight Arsenal all the way for the fourth Champions League qualifying spot. This was not how it was supposed to be, thought Cesc. The pressure was on, but the Spaniard had always produced his best displays when it mattered most and he continued to impress everyone with his decision-making on the pitch.

Manchester United had also found it impossible to keep up with Chelsea. While they were not as far adrift as Cesc and his team-mates, Ferguson's side needed a miracle to overtake Mourinho's rampant squad. Strangely, United's clash with Arsenal at Highbury on 3 January was missing some of its usual bite with both sides still coming to terms with the Blues' remarkable title surge. It felt odd that neither club was in serious contention after all the battles in the late nineties and early years of the new millennium. The absences of Roy Keane, who left United in late 2005, and Vieira were hard to get used to.

The match came at the end of a hectic Christmas schedule and it was hardly surprising that it finished 0-0. Both sides had a number of chances, but nobody had the composure or energy to find the net. A weary Fábregas lasted eighty minutes and was involved in one of the game's key moments as he fell in the area after Gary Neville's sliding tackle. The England defender appeared to take man and ball, but referee Graham Poll waved away the penalty claims. Replays suggested the Spaniard might have had good reason to feel aggrieved. The result left a broad smile on Mourinho's face as Chelsea's lead at the top stretched to thirteen points. But the result did not only leave Chelsea fans rejoicing. On the other side of North London, Tottenham supporters watched in delight as the Gunners dropped yet more points in the race for fourth place. These were worrying times at Highbury.

Wenger tried to keep calm when addressing the media after the match and pointed to the challenge on Fábregas as a key moment: 'We wanted to win, but it was a high pace and I felt both teams were always trying to have a break to get the other on the counter attack. I felt it was very close to a penalty on Fábregas when Neville tackled him from behind in the area.' In truth, a draw was probably a fair result. Ferguson agreed.

The FA Cup provided a welcome distraction for the Gunners. But their 2-1 victory over Cardiff at Highbury on 7 January was not always comfortable as the visitors pulled a goal back late on and threatened to grab an unlikely equaliser in the dying moments of the game. Fábregas was rested for the match along with a handful of other stars, but it only gave him time to reflect on the team's mixed results. He was a frustrated substitute again in midweek as Arsenal suffered a 1-0 defeat at Wigan in the first leg of their Carling Cup semi-final. Cesc got eighteen minutes of action, but could do nothing to prevent the outcome. The competition represented a chance of silverware, even if it was mainly the club's youngsters who appeared in it.

On 14 January, football fans all over the country were reminded of how good Fábregas and company could be on their day as Arsenal thrashed Middlesbrough 7-0 at Highbury. It was an incredible match which raised questions of why the Gunners did not produce the same level of clinical finishing on a more regular basis. Cesc went close to joining in with the goalscoring, but was denied by Boro goalkeeper Brad Jones. Henry struck a hat-trick as the home fans were treated to a masterclass in slick, attacking football. It was a joy to watch.

But a week later, a 1-0 loss at Everton underlined the reason why Arsenal were trailing the other top clubs. Fábregas and his team-mates could not string together good performances, especially away from Highbury. The Toffees worked harder and showed more desire, winning thanks to an early goal from James Beattie. Cesc toiled in midfield, but found himself frequently frustrated by tenacious Everton challenges. It all boiled over for the Spaniard in the closing moments. With Tim Cahill and Henry squaring up, Fábregas rushed over and threw himself at the Everton midfielder, leaving referee Alan Wiley with no choice but to produce a red card. Wenger was livid, telling the media: 'Away from home we have a problem. We always lose 1-0 and we need to find a response by the end of the season to finish in the top four.' Fábregas would now face a three-match suspension.

Cesc had to content himself with watching a few matches from the sidelines. It made for painful viewing. In midweek, Wigan snatched a last-gasp goal to eliminate Arsenal in the Carling Cup semi-final second leg, just as it looked as though the Gunners had booked their place in the final. It denied Fábregas the chance to return to the Millennium Stadium and ended the team's participation in another competition. Worse followed as Bolton knocked Arsenal out of the FA Cup at the Reebok Stadium on 28 January. The Spaniard was disappointed that his ban prevented him from helping his team-mates.

Much had been made of how Arsenal were struggling without the departed Vieira, but not enough was said about how the Gunners missed Fábregas during his suspension. Dumped out of two cup competitions in a matter of days, Wenger looked miserable. How he would have loved to have had Cesc available to him. With the Spaniard still banned, Arsenal were lurching from one disaster to the next. At home to West Ham, things took another turn for the worst. Defensive errors from Sol Campbell allowed the Hammers to take a two-goal lead and the Gunners could not recover, losing 3-2. As

Fábregas sat stunned, his hopes of playing in next year's Champions League appeared to be going up in smoke.

Sandwiched between the defeats to Bolton and West Ham, Cesc received thrilling news when he was called up to the Spanish senior squad for the first time for the friendly against the Ivory Coast. It was a well-deserved opportunity for the youngster and improved his mood during his three-match suspension. He told *Marca* newspaper: 'It is a very special day for me because it is the first time that I am joining up with the squad. If I am lucky enough to make my debut, it will be very exciting.' Assuming Fábregas gave a good account of himself, there was still time for him to compete for a place in the Spanish World Cup squad. Typically understated, the youngster told the press: 'I can only say that I am very happy. I am going to give it everything.'

It was little surprise that Cesc's return from suspension coincided with Arsenal's improved form. The team had lacked his calm presence in midfield and his ability to spot the right pass at the right time. Goals from Adebayor and Henry sealed a 2-0 victory away to Birmingham as the Gunners tried to build some momentum ahead of the Champions League second round. The draw had not been kind to Fábregas and his team-mates as they were paired with Spanish giants Real Madrid, who have such a rich history in the competition. As a Barcelona supporter, it would be an emotional tie for Cesc. He hoped his side's fragile confidence could stand up to the challenge.

The tie would allow Fábregas to fulfil one of his childhood dreams – playing at the Santiago Bernabeu, the home of Real Madrid. Cesc had faced Real at youth level during his time at Barcelona, but never inside the famous stadium. He told *Marca*: 'Neither me nor many of the Arsenal players have played in the Bernabeu. I have enormous excitement about playing in Madrid. On a personal level, I know that I have an extraordinary opportunity to offer the Spanish public the [type of] football that the English people already know.' He also acknowledged that it should be a great showcase of attacking football, as both sides liked to play positively, with the emphasis on attack rather than defence. It seemed destined to be a high-scoring affair.

Facing Real Madrid meant a lot more for Fábregas than just simply a tricky second-round match-up. The game in the Bernabeu would be his first on Spanish soil since leaving Barcelona in 2003 and he was eager to show the people out there how far he had come in the interceding years. He was not, however, kidding himself about the reaction he might receive from the home crowd, being an opponent *and* a Barça fan. Cesc told the *Independent* in mid-February: 'I will be their rival, so I will try to win for Arsenal and for myself – and, of course, they won't say nice things about me.'

His friends back in Catalonia could not stop talking about the tie and it all contributed to a rather surreal feeling for Cesc. While, like so many teenagers, Fábregas often chatted on MSN Messenger, the subject matter of his conversations with his mates – passionate Barcelona supporters – was far from typical of teenage life. Cesc and his friends were discussing the youngster's role against Real Madrid in the Champions League. It was incredible and there were times when Fábregas had to pinch himself to believe it was not a dream.

The Spaniard told the *Independent*: 'When they talk to me on MSN Messenger they are just saying, "Come on, beat them, beat them." They are going mad about it. It's going to be just one more game, but a big game, a special game because Real Madrid – you don't play them every day.' His friends back home would be cheering him on, but it would be a different story later in the season.

Domestically, Bolton again proved to be a thorn in Arsenal's side, drawing 1-1 with the Gunners at Highbury and coming within seconds of taking all three points. Luckily for Wenger, Fábregas never stopped running and his never-say-die attitude salvaged a point for the team. His cross found Gilberto and the Brazilian struck home the equaliser. Even this drama could not stir Arsenal into life. Just a week before the first leg of the tie with Real Madrid, Cesc and his team-mates lost again – this time at Anfield against Liverpool. It did not bode well for their trip to Spain.

As Fábregas was well aware, the beauty of football is its endless ability to surprise people and overturn the formbook. Considering the Gunners' recent form, Real were the firm favourites for the Champions League clash – but nobody doubted the quality in the Arsenal line-up. Could they produce a magical performance on the big stage? Could they silence the Bernabeu? It would be a big ask.

Despite some negative media coverage, the Gunners travelled to Madrid in high spirits. The Champions League was the only trophy left for Fábregas and company and they were determined to fight for it. This meant putting recent results to one side and focusing on the 180 minutes ahead. Their opponents boasted *galacticos* such as Ronaldo, David Beckham, Zinedine Zidane, Roberto Carlos and Raúl, but Arsenal had stars of their own – and Cesc was one of them.

Most neutrals gave the Gunners little chance of getting a result away from home, but it turned out to be a sensational night for the Gunners; a night that pulled the team closer together; a night that convinced Cesc once and for all that he belonged on the biggest stage. Partnering Gilberto in central midfield, the Spaniard gave an assured performance as Arsenal achieved the unthinkable. They won in Real Madrid's backyard.

After a goalless first half, in which the Gunners always looked dangerous, Fábregas came out positively for the second period, knowing that Madrid were there for the taking. The Spanish side appeared shaky in defence and Wenger urged his players to be positive. Henry produced the perfect response, gliding past several Real challenges before slotting the ball past goalkeeper Iker Casillas. The Bernabeu was stunned into silence and Cesc and his team-mates truly believed victory was possible. Strong defending and plenty of energetic midfield work helped the Gunners protect their lead and Fábregas even had the audacity to employ a Cruyff turn to outwit his marker near the halfway line late in the game as he turned on the style. When he was substituted in the dying moments, the Spaniard received a great ovation from all sections of the crowd.

It was a massive moment in Arsenal's season. After all the erratic performances, the players had put in a superb shift just at the right time. A new resilience seemed to appear in the side when they took to the field in Champions League matches and Fábregas hoped this would lead to a lengthy run towards the latter stages of the competition. However, he refused to get carried away. The 1-0 win in Madrid may have been a phenomenal achievement, but the job was only half finished.

Wenger struggled to hide his emotions after the match, telling the media: 'The young players did well. There was not a single player who wasn't outstanding. We started well and that may have made Real insecure. I'm happy in every department.'

Henry was equally thrilled and praised the slick passing that had enabled the Gunners to pick holes in the Madrid back four: 'You can see that as soon as Arsenal are not scared to play, we can play good football. In some games recently we have been kicking the ball up front for no reason. Here we played football.' No doubt, Fábregas' return from suspension had helped with the improved build-up play. In the Bernabeu, his touch and vision had been outstanding and once again he had displayed a level of maturity well beyond his years.

The Real Madrid boss Juan Ramon Lopez Caro grudgingly praised the way Gilberto and Fábregas had patrolled the midfield and denied their Madrid counterparts time on the ball: 'We never really managed to find any clarity or precision in midfield and didn't show our usual personality.' Caro had unleashed an array of attackers as the home side desperately sought an equaliser, but the Gunners were able to hold firm.

Beckham was equally gracious in defeat and picked out Cesc as one of Arsenal's top performers: 'It was very difficult against players like Henry, Reyes, Fábregas. We were very bad and they were superior.' The England captain, though, maintained that the tie was not over and that Madrid would be looking for revenge at Highbury.

The next day, the Spanish newspapers focused in on Cesc's display and the English media were quick to reflect on their Spanish counterparts' appreciation for Cesc. As Amy Lawrence of the *Guardian* explained: 'In his [Fábregas'] first match as a professional footballer in his homeland he had earned the instant respect of his compatriots. The next day's newspapers were effusive.' Indeed they were. Madrid-based *AS* praised the Arsenal scouts who had tempted Cesc away from Barça while the media in Barcelona mocked Real's incompetent display and took pride in the fact that Fábregas had been educated at their *cantera*.

As Lawrence pointed out, if Barcelona had been more alert, they could have held onto Cesc. She wrote: 'Local pride in Fábregas' development is one thing, but it is a sore point for Barcelona that he left to make the grade. The story exposes how difficult it is to balance developing youngsters with signing experienced players. Fábregas has already played almost 100 games for Arsenal and he appreciates the equality he enjoyed at Highbury from day one, saying: "I never trained with the first team at Barcelona, but I've spoken to Messi. He says if you do something wrong, everyone says, "He's young, it's OK." It's not like that here [at Arsenal]. Here you're treated like all the other players.'"

The victory in Madrid left the Gunners exhausted, but content. However, the tired legs showed at Ewood Park against Blackburn at the weekend as Fábregas and his colleagues failed to match Rovers' intensity and lost 1-0. It was hardly surprising considering the ecstasy of the midweek triumph, but Cesc knew the team could not afford to become complacent in their bid to claim fourth place.

There was barely time for Fábregas to take in the defeat before he headed to Valladolid for one of the biggest occasions of his brief career to date. Ever since he had heard the news of his call-up to the Spanish senior squad, Cesc had been looking forward to the country's friendly against the Ivory Coast. Even though it was the youngster's first call-up, manager Luis Aragones had no doubts about throwing the youngster into the fray, picking Cesc in a four-man midfield. It was a tremendous moment for him and it sparked celebrations in his home town. His family were so proud as Fábregas stepped out onto the field for his first cap, wearing the number eight shirt. In the process, he became the second youngest player in Spain's history to represent the national team.

The Ivorians were no pushovers, though, and boasted the likes of Didier Drogba. An end-to-end game – in which Spain trailed twice – ended 3-2 to the Spaniards and it ensured Cesc's debut was even more memorable. He made the key contribution for the team's opening goal, scored by David Villa, and was one of the success stories on the night for Spain. The media raved about his performance. Fábregas told the press: 'I am happy with how it all went and, even better, we won. It's one of the happiest days of my life. I played well and the crowd and coach helped me a lot. It was a busy week, but very special.'

Back in Premiership action, Fábregas knew that Arsenal had to improve on their recent domestic form by finding some consistency. A more fluent, confident display came against Fulham at Craven Cottage on 4 March. With one eye on the second leg of their Champions League fixture against Real Madrid in midweek, Wenger left Fábregas on the bench, but the youngster came on for the final ten minutes and scored the team's fourth goal in a 4-0 victory.

It was the best possible preparation for Real's visit. With Beckham returning to play in England for the first time since his move to Madrid in 2003, all eyes were on Highbury. Again Real sent out a team packed with international stars and again Arsenal held firm. Lehmann was forced to make several vital stops, but for the most part Cesc and his team-mates kept the visitors at bay. It should have been a nervy time for Fábregas, considering his age and the knife-edge nature of the contest, but he got on with his job with the minimum of fuss. The only sign of any nerves came when he missed a decent first-half chance.

Showing the commitment that had been missing too often in Premiership outings, Arsenal defended manfully and Real could not break through. The final whistle blew and Fábregas and company had done it. They had knocked out the great Real Madrid and had proved many people wrong in the process. The players soaked up the applause from the crowd and the Gunners' celebrations went on long into the night. Their season was very much alive and it seemed that having all their eggs in the Champions League basket was having a fantastic effect on their displays in Europe. The spirit and commitment was phenomenal. Fábregas and his team-mates were playing to save their campaign every night in Europe and it was bringing out the best in them.

Cesc's individual performances across the two legs of the tie, in front of hordes of Spanish viewers back home, had enhanced his chances of snatching a place in the

Spanish World Cup squad. The target had become a realistic one. If he kept playing this well, Aragones would be mad not to pick the youngster. After witnessing his brilliance and maturity against Real, there was no doubt the Spanish public would be calling for Fábregas to go to Germany.

Wenger was jubilant and told the press: 'To play two games against Real and not concede a goal shows remarkable spirit. Something is happening with this team. They are gelling together. They have shown character, and that is very good. I feel we have grown as a team during these last two months.' Nobody seemed to have grown in stature more than Fábregas, who had relished the big-match atmosphere and had really come of age during the past six months.

It was hard to describe the boost victory over Real had given the club, but the results over the following few weeks at least partly told the story. Having meekly surrendered to Liverpool at Anfield on 14 February, Arsenal made amends on 12 March with a 2-1 home win over Benitez's side. The Gunners displayed plenty of spirit, but needed a helping hand from Liverpool captain Steven Gerrard, who set up Henry's winner with a poor backpass. Earlier in the campaign, Cesc and company might only have drawn such a contest; now they had the courage and belief to grind out victories.

Charlton were the next to suffer, losing 3-0 at Highbury on 18 March. Fábregas played the majority of the match and was grateful not to be rested. He was on such a high at the moment – he just wanted to keep the momentum going. The Gunners then had a ten-day break to prepare for the first leg of their Champions

League quarter-final against Fabio Capello's Juventus. It would be another huge test for Wenger's youthful side, but Cesc looked forward to the tie with excitement. The Arsenal players had got the better of Beckham and Zidane; now they would face Pavel Nedved, David Trezeguet and, of course, their old team-mate Patrick Vieira. Now everyone would see how much the Gunners were really missing Vieira.

It proved to be another incredible European night, especially for Fábregas. Lining up alongside Gilberto again in midfield, Cesc was fired up as he felt the passion of the Arsenal fans and set out to limit Vieira's midfield influence. Highbury was rocking. From the first whistle, the Gunners launched into the visitors, giving them no time to settle. Fábregas chose this night to produce one of his best-ever displays, working hard to win possession and distributing the ball confidently. His big moment came just before half-time. Pires made a brilliant challenge on Vieira, Henry collected the loose ball and found Cesc. The Spaniard worked an opening against French international Lilian Thuram and drilled the ball past goalkeeper Gianluigi Buffon into the bottom corner. The ground erupted. Vieira gingerly got to his feet as the crowd jeered. After all the comments about the Frenchman's summer exit, it was somehow symbolic that he was the man who had been dispossessed in the build-up to the goal – fans were witnessing the changing of the guard. Maybe this would stop the criticism of Wenger's decision to sell the midfielder.

Fábregas was involved in another slick move in the second half as Arsenal looked to kill off their opponents. He was not tracked by the Juventus midfield and found himself through on goal. Never one to panic in crucial moments, he shaped to shoot, only to lay the ball across towards Henry. The pass was a little behind the French striker, but with Buffon stranded by Cesc's disguised ball, Henry was able to roll a shot into the net. 2-0. The Italians were rattled. Vieira was booked and then two Juventus players were sent off in the final few minutes. At the final whistle, Fábregas basked in the glory of the moment. He had been sensational at the heart of everything the Gunners had done. Suddenly the headlines were focused on the merits of the 'new generation' at Arsenal and how far they could go in the competition. Vieira and Juventus had been slow and laboured; the Gunners had displayed a youthful swagger.

Post-match, all the talk surrounded the diminutive Spaniard. Henry told the media: 'Cesc is doing extremely well. If you let him play he can kill a team. I think you see more of him when we play five in the middle. He knew today that he had Gilberto behind him. He knows when to go into the box, when to join and when he had time on the ball.' Wenger also saluted the way that the youngsters had played: 'They [the players] are not inhibited. There is quality in this team and they are good to watch. It wasn't my target tonight to justify selling Patrick. But another team was born and is growing slowly. Football is like that.' One more goal would have put the tie to bed for Arsenal, but Juventus still had a glimmer of a chance and Fábregas knew that the players would have to do it all again in Turin to secure a place in the semi-final. Defying the expectations of many was incredibly satisfying.

Cesc was buzzing with excitement. The team was

brimming with confidence again and carried their European form into their next Premiership fixture at home to Aston Villa, who were unfortunate to catch the Gunners in sublime form as Wenger's side racked up a fine 5-0 win. However, it was not such a memorable day for Fábregas, who pulled up with an injury and had to leave the field after just fifteen minutes. With the return match against Juventus in midweek, the Spaniard faced a race against time to be fit for the trip to Italy.

As if there was ever any chance of him missing the game! Cesc had worked too hard simply to sit and watch as the Gunners fought for a Champions League semi-final slot. His injury improved in the days after the Villa match and Fábregas had no doubts about whether he would be fit in time to face Juventus. Wenger was a relieved man to hear the Spaniard declare himself available. It seemed destined to be a nail-biting night in Turin.

Wenger sent out a defensive line-up, but the Gunners always looked dangerous with the passing range of Fábregas and the pace of Henry. With Pires on the bench and Bergkamp not travelling, Cesc stepped up again to show he could handle the playmaking responsibilities. Czech international Pavel Nedved, who had missed the first leg, was Juventus' biggest threat, but the defence stood up to the challenge. Fábregas had a terrific chance on the counter attack, but Buffon saved well. The expected nervous finale never arrived and the Gunners had done it again. The European run continued and a semi-final clash against Spanish side Villarreal awaited.

After the game, emotions ran wild as the players began to realise just how far they had come over the past few months. Arsène Wenger told the media: 'We are very proud – two months ago no-one expected that from our players. This year we have knocked out Real Madrid and Juventus and, of course, now we have a big appetite and we want to play well in the semi-final against Villarreal.' The Champions League had seen the Gunners produce some of their most heroic and exhilarating performances of the season and the travelling Arsenal supporters were jubilant.

Considering the emotional rollercoaster ride of the past few weeks, it was hardly surprising that the Gunners could not lift themselves away to a resurgent Manchester United, who were attempting to put pressure on Chelsea. Arsenal gave it their all, but their weary legs just could not compete with the home side and the exhaustion really began to show in the second half as United took the lead through Wayne Rooney and, after Cesc had been replaced, doubled their advantage thanks to a Ji-Sung Park goal. Though annoyed at losing to such fierce rivals, Fábregas knew he could have done no more for the cause.

There were bigger issues for Arsenal to deal with anyway. Not only their upcoming Champions League semi-final, but also their farewell to Highbury. With the Emirates Stadium set to be ready for the start of the 2006/07 season, Cesc only had a few more home matches to savour the special atmosphere at Highbury – the only English ground he had ever known. Still, there would be big celebrations to remember all the amazing nights that they had had at the old stadium. Perhaps there would be a couple more before the move too.

Wenger gave Fábregas a chance to rest his injured foot

during the 1-1 draw away to Portsmouth. Cesc had been carrying the knock since the 5-0 win over Aston Villa and Arsène felt it was time he aided the Spaniard's recovery, albeit to the detriment of the team. Without Fábregas, the Gunners were frustrated by Pompey and the draw meant that Arsenal were now in serious danger of missing out on fourth place. It was now out of their hands. Tottenham had refused to cave in and panic began to spread around the Gunners' dressing room at the thought of missing out on Champions League football the following season.

Cesc was also left out of the team that beat West Brom 3-1 at Highbury on 15 April. While Wenger would have liked to rest several more big names for the midweek clash with Villarreal, he could not afford his team to lose more ground on Spurs. The Frenchman was not optimistic of Fábregas' chances of being fit to face the Spanish outfit: 'There is a little chance. But he had a recurrence of the injury. It is a worry, and we want to clear the problem completely. At the moment it is not clear.' The Gunners boss also took the chance to put forward his votes for the PFA Player and Young Player of the Year awards: 'My list is very short. It is Thierry Henry and Cesc Fábregas – and by miles. You cannot see anyone coming close to them.'

Whether Arsène had just been employing some mind games ahead of the Villarreal clash, it was hard to tell. But in the end Fábregas was indeed fit to start the game. The first leg was at Highbury and Cesc urged the home fans to make it an intimidating arena for the visitors, who were strangers to this stage of European football. If he and his team-mates could win by a couple of goals, it would give the team some breathing space for the return match. Though never flustered, even Fábregas felt the grandeur of the occasion and could not wait to get out onto the pitch.

Part of a five-man midfield, Cesc worked hard for space in the congested area. The Gunners put Villarreal on the back foot and finally took advantage just before half-time as Kolo Toure scrambled the ball home. The visitors, though, did not crumble. Fábregas, playing through the pain, helped create several good opportunities, but their opponents also forced Lehmann into some smart stops. In the end, Arsenal had to settle for a 1-0 victory. It was a solid result, especially as Villarreal had failed to register an away goal, but the tie was still very much alive and Arsenal would have to be in good form to secure their place in the Champions League final – Villarreal had an excellent home record.

Wenger implored his players not to dwell on the good midweek win and to focus on beating Tottenham the following weekend in the last North London derby of the season, at Highbury. It was a crucial one, too. Cesc and his colleagues needed a win to aid their chances of snatching fourth place, while defeat could bring that pursuit to a heartbreaking end. Arsène bravely opted to leave Fábregas and Henry on the bench for the game with one eye on the trip to Spain the following Tuesday. And he almost paid the price.

Both Cesc and Henry were sent on after sixty-two minutes with the game scoreless. Shortly after, Tottenham took the lead in dubious circumstances. Emmanuel Eboué was down injured yet Spurs did not put the ball out of play to allow the defender to receive treatment.

Instead, unaware of the injury, they played on and scored through Robbie Keane. Wenger and the Arsenal players were furious and confronted their Tottenham counterparts. It looked like being a major moment in a huge game. A late equaliser from Henry salvaged a point from the match, but Arsène was still fuming after the game, clashing with Spurs boss Martin Jol and ranting about the incident in front of the media. Cesc had rarely seen his manager so animated – perhaps Wenger was in part regretting his decision to leave his two biggest stars on the bench.

Having missed the perfect chance to close in on their fourth-placed neighbours, the Gunners turned their attention back to their midweek Champions League match as they travelled to Spain for a huge ninety minutes of football. It was a nerve-racking night for everyone associated with Arsenal, but the players themselves kept cool heads, despite constant Villarreal pressure. It was not really Fábregas' type of match, as he and his team-mates spent much of the game scrapping for possession and breaking up attacks. But the youngster gave his all in midfield, supporting the tireless Gilberto and helping to relieve the tension with careful passing. This match was all about stamina and desire – plans for attractive football went out of the window.

On the night, the Gunners had reason to be eternally thankful to Lehmann, who kept up his fine run of form. Real Madrid and Juventus had not found a way past him and nor could Villarreal. On the occasions when Arsenal's defence was breeched, the German stopper was on hand to make a string of crucial saves. Then, with Arsenal clinging on desperately and with only seconds to go, their worst nightmare materialised in front of their eyes. Full-back Gael Clichy challenged Villarreal forward Jose Mari and referee Ivan Ivanov stunned the Gunners by awarding a penalty to the home side. After all the hard graft, a dubious decision by an official had given the Spaniards a last-gasp chance to get out of jail.

Argentine Juan Roman Riquelme, Villarreal's star man, took the penalty, but Lehmann produced one last heroic contribution, guessing the right way and saving the spot-kick. His colleagues mobbed him. Arsenal could breathe again! They survived the last seconds before Ivanov blew the whistle, to send the Gunners to Paris for the Champions League final. Fábregas was overcome with emotion. It may not have been his finest performance for the club, but it had been one of the most rewarding and memorable. A season that for so long appeared destined to end in misery, now had the potential for a grand finale.

Wenger told the media post-match: 'We were lucky, but I'm very proud of the character in that young team and I'm very happy. We showed such character. Now we are in the final, we want to win. We have had a great European season and now we want to finish it off.'

The following evening, Barcelona narrowly held off the challenge of AC Milan to book their place in the final. Cesc would be facing his childhood team in the biggest game of his career. It made the occasion even more special. It was sure to be a very emotional night for Fábregas and his family.

As the pursuit of fourth place entered the crucial final stages, Arsène did not dare to rest his big-name players. Therefore, just days after the momentous night in Spain, Fábregas was back in action away to Sunderland. Wenger was relieved to see his side wrap up the points in the first half, scoring three times and outclassing their feeble opponents, who were heading back to the Championship with a record low points total. Cesc grabbed the Gunners' second goal, benefiting from Henry's powerful run and leaving Black Cats goalkeeper Kelvin Davis with no chance. Wenger made changes in the second half, but the Spaniard stayed out on the pitch and soaked up the applause after the final whistle.

Tottenham were showing signs of faltering and Arsenal were ready and waiting. A 3-1 victory at Manchester City on 4 May – Fábregas' birthday – cranked up the pressure another notch. Cesc was named among the substitutes and helped to clinch the win during a half-hour cameo appearance. Spurs' lead had been cut to just one point going into the final weekend of the Premiership season. Fábregas and company just had to better Tottenham's result and then their gutsy comeback would be complete.

It set up a mouth-watering finale for Arsenal's last game at Highbury. Nobody could have scripted it better. Cesc and his team-mates had given the old stadium a terrific European run and now the squad prepared to finish on a high. Wigan were their opponents – the side who had eliminated the Gunners from the Carling Cup semi-final in such agonising fashion earlier in the season. Meanwhile, Tottenham faced West Ham. Arsenal supporters would be keeping a close eye on proceedings at Upton Park all afternoon.

With a ten-day break between the Wigan fixture and the Champions League final, Wenger did not worry about resting players. He selected a full-strength side and, although the visitors did their best to spoil the party, going 2-1 up just after the half hour mark, ultimately it was Arsenal's day. Fábregas was heavily involved in the team's best moves and enjoyed the atmosphere of the occasion. Henry scored a hat-trick and the Gunners picked up a 4-2 victory, giving Highbury the perfect send-off. At full-time, news filtered through that West Ham had beaten Tottenham, who had suffered as food poisoning swept through the squad. Arsenal had snatched fourth place. There was a sense of relief as much as celebration.

It was an emotional end to the Highbury era and Cesc could only feel sad to be leaving such a special stadium. He thought back to his first Arsenal goal, scored there at Highbury, and his home Premiership debut. The ground held many important memories for him and he would not forget it. There was a strange mixture of sadness and joy that afternoon as the curtain came down on the Gunners' famous old stadium.

His team-mates felt the same way. Henry explained to the press: 'We've missed so many players this season and we did it the hard way. When I kissed the ground after my third [goal], I was saying goodbye to this stadium.' Wenger added: 'For the history of the club and for this building here, to finish on a high I am very proud. We would all have felt guilty to have walked out of here on a low after what has happened here for years.'

It was difficult for Fábregas to know what to do in the build-up to the Champions League final. The ten-day gap was frustrating as he just wanted to get out there and play. On the other hand, though, it gave his body a rest. It had been a long season for the youngster – with only a few breaks – and it was vital that he took proper care of himself. He could rest his foot and get back into peak condition.

As the squad headed for Paris, the excitement grew and grew. Cesc had enjoyed a brilliant campaign so far, but playing in the Champions League final was a clear highlight. He tried to concentrate on it as just another match in order to keep his feet on the ground and his nerves under control. Barcelona boasted a star-studded side, including Fábregas' *cantera* colleague Messi, Samuel Eto'o and the great Brazilian Ronaldinho. But Wenger hoped the Catalan giants were just as wary of the talent of Cesc, Henry and Pires.

Naturally, Fábregas was besieged with demands from the media prior to the game. It would be an emotional night. He had always dreamed of winning a European final with Barcelona; now he was playing against them on the biggest stage. It was the type of story the media thrived on. Cesc remained calm when speaking to the press and joked about how his friends back home had suddenly become a bit less supportive of his career! Fábregas and Messi had gone toe-to-toe on the international scene in the Under-17 and Under-21 World Cups. They had a win each. This match, though, was the biggest game either of them had ever appeared in.

He told reporters: 'It's a funny situation. When I'm in England they [his friends] say "good luck", then you face Barcelona and everyone says "please don't play well". I'm from near Barcelona and I can tell you the pressure [on them] is very high. They have been trying to win it since 1992 and they have lost three finals. But for us it is our first time and we can make it one out of one. It can be the best thing for Arsenal. I spent six years at Barça. I learned a lot of things and I have a lot of friends – not just team-mates but coaches as well so, of course, it will be very special for me. But I know exactly what I want and that is winning for Arsenal.'

However, Henry's long-term commitment to the club was less certain. It looked more and more likely he would move to Barcelona in the summer.

Fábregas could not wait for the Champions League final and sent out a rallying cry to his team-mates: 'Barcelona are beatable. Yes, they are a great team – they have shown that over the last two years – and it is going to be difficult. But it has been like that all through the competition. Against Madrid we were not the favourites and against Juventus we were not the favourites. And I hope it will continue.' The 'underdogs' tag suited the Gunners. While everyone concentrated on Barcelona's attacking triumvirate, Cesc and his colleagues were able to get on with their own preparations.

Arsenal continued with the 4-5-1 formation that had helped the team reach the final. Fábregas and Gilberto would be responsible for stopping Barcelona's midfield from dominating possession and Cesc would always be looking for Henry's runs in behind the Barça back line. Walking out and feeling the atmosphere inside the stadium, even just for the warm-up, was an incredible sensation for Fábregas and he soaked up every minute of it. This was the type of match he was born to play in.

However, after all the ecstasy of the occasion, the anthems and the team photo, Arsenal suffered a cruel blow in the eighteenth minute of the game when

Lehmann was red-carded for bringing down Eto'o just outside the area. It was a disastrous moment after what had been a promising start from the Gunners. Pires was sacrificed as Manuel Almunia took over in goal. From then on it was always going to be an uphill struggle for Cesc and his team-mates. It would have been hard enough to subdue Barcelona with eleven men.

But the Gunners dug deep and fought for their lives. Fábregas got through a mountain of work in midfield, denying the likes of Ronaldinho and Messi the freedom to punish Arsenal. Then, to everyone's surprise, the ten men took the lead. Emmanuel Eboué, the Ivorian right-back signed in January, won a free-kick on the right and Henry's delivery was powered home by Campbell, who was only back in the side due to an injury to Senderos. Could Cesc and company really pull this off? Would it be yet another incredible chapter in this European story? The Gunners fans certainly hoped so. They were on their feet as the ball hit the back of the net and the players rushed over to celebrate. They believed it too.

Gritty defending and good goalkeeping from Almunia saw Arsenal take their 1-0 lead into the half-time interval. Wenger looked a proud man, but urged his team to stay focused. As the rain fell, the Gunners began to sense this might be their night and the game became increasingly scrappy. Barcelona threw men forward in search of an equaliser and a weary Henry came close to punishing them. A second goal would have clinched the game.

Wenger decided to bring on Flamini to replace Fábregas for the final fifteen minutes, feeling that the Spaniard had given everything to the cause and thinking that fresh legs might make the difference in defending the slender lead. Instead, Barcelona soon made the breakthrough. Cesc watched in dismay as substitute Henrik Larsson found Eto'o and the Cameroonian striker beat Almunia at his near post. It came two minutes after Fábregas was taken off. The youngster was devastated as he sat helplessly on the bench, watching the trophy slipping out of the team's hands.

Worse was to follow. Larsson was again involved as fellow substitute Juliano Belletti burst forward and broke Arsenal hearts. His shot nestled in the net and Barça breathed a huge sigh of relief as they celebrated a dramatic turnaround – two goals in four minutes. The Gunners had been floored. They had nothing left in the tank and Barcelona hung on to their advantage to win 2-1. Cesc was distraught. While he understood the thinking behind the substitution, he was hugely disappointed that he had not been out there to help his team-mates – perhaps he could have made a difference. He would never know.

The Arsenal players were very bitter after the game, feeling robbed and cheated by the officials. Fábregas told the press: 'You have to be fair in football – you have to be honest and well done to you if you've won, but you have to win in a good way. I don't like to be in the position of saying things about the referee, but maybe it's true. If you look at the first goal for Barça, it's clearly offside.' Cesc was also furious at the treatment received by Henry from defenders Rafael Marquez and Carlos Puyol – a topic the French striker discussed at great length with the media after the match.

It was a horrible way to lose and it would take some

time before Fábregas got over the pain of this defeat. The runners-up medal was not what he had come for and the Arsenal players could not have looked more aggrieved when they went forward to the podium and had to walk past the trophy. It was a gloomy way for Cesc's season to end. After all the hype, all the plaudits and all the media attention, he and his team-mates had ended the season empty-handed. He knew this was not acceptable for a club of Arsenal's stature.

But he had plenty of high points to look back on, even if the Gunners had been below par too often in the Premiership. Fábregas had played a key role in helping Arsenal reach the Champions League final and had been a driving force in the domestic turnaround that saw the team clinch fourth spot with a strong finish to the campaign. Wenger had increasingly come to rely on Cesc to influence matches and make vital contributions. The Spaniard had shown no fear on the big occasions and looked set to feature in the starting line-up for years to come. Arsenal fans were not quite asking 'Patrick who?', but Fábregas had given them plenty of reasons to be positive about the future.

For Cesc, though, the season was not over. He had to put the disappointments of the domestic campaign behind him and focus on the next challenge, because Aragones and Spain would be relying on him. The European adventure was about to go global.

CHAPTER 4

THE WORLD CUP DREAM AND THE START OF THE EMIRATES ERA

At nineteen years of age, Fábregas was ready for the next chapter of his incredible story. The Champions League journey had been a tremendous experience, but now it was time to focus on the international stage. His inclusion in the Spain squad for the 2006 World Cup had come as a massive boost and spoke volumes for his development as a player. While he had hoped his performances deserved selection, it was a great relief to receive the good news from Aragones and see his name on the list for the competition in Germany. It was an emotional day and his family were thrilled for him. It would be a tense summer in Cesc's home town.

He had made no secret of his desire to play in the tournament, telling the Spanish media: 'The World Cup is a dream for me. It is the greatest recognition a footballer can have and it would be incredible to be in Germany with the squad.' But he could understand why he might miss out: 'The truth is I am very young and I know that there is difficulty because there is a lot of talent. I have my feet on the ground.' However, with his seat on the plane to Germany confirmed, Fábregas could look forward to an exciting summer with his international colleagues.

Spain had made hard work of reaching the tournament. Drawn in Group Seven along with Belgium, Serbia and Montenegro, Bosnia and Herzegovina, Lithuania and San Marino, the Spanish squad had laboured. At this stage, of course, Cesc was simply an interested spectator. He had not yet even received his first cap and was more interested in cementing a place in the Arsenal first team before he could think about the international scene.

Though Spain did not lose a match in their qualifying campaign, they drew five of their ten matches and allowed Serbia and Montenegro to top the group by two points. This forced the Spaniards into a high-stakes play-off against Slovakia, which they won comfortably. Their performances in Germany would have to be better.

Fábregas had watched avidly – and nervously at times – as Spain clinched their spot in the tournament. When qualification had been confirmed on 16 November 2005, Cesc was just months into his second season in the Arsenal first team and, though he has never lacked ambition, he could not have anticipated bursting into the national team squad in time for the World Cup.

But he had done it and his selection for the tournament showed his incredible progress. Cesc had only made his debut for the Spanish senior side against the Ivory Coast in February and yet he had leapfrogged a host of other celebrated players to secure his inclusion in the squad.

His impact had been so immediate he had forced his way into Aragones' plans within the space of a few months and even fewer matches. It would have been easy for Fábregas to be content to be part of the squad, but he had higher targets. Wayne Rooney had shot to fame in similar fashion for England at Euro 2004. The striker, then at Everton, had been thrown into the first team for a big qualifier against Turkey and had never looked back. By the time Sven-Göran Eriksson came to pick his squad for that tournament, Rooney was a certainty. He, like Fábregas in 2006, had made himself undroppable.

Spain, like most nations, played a string of warm-up friendlies prior to the tournament to finish off preparations for the event. Cesc was eager to perform well and make a good impression on his manager, Aragones. First, on 27 May, the Spaniards drew 0-0 with Russia. Fábregas started the match, but was substituted at half-time to give Andres Iniesta a chance to stake his claim. It was not the most entertaining of matches and the players looked weary after long European seasons. They would have to raise the tempo if they wanted to last long in Germany but, of course, the adrenalin rush of a big tournament would soon kick in.

On 3 June, the Spaniards beat Egypt 2-0 in Elche in a much-improved display with Raul and Cesc's Arsenal team-mate Reyes grabbing the goals. Fábregas was given a starting role again alongside David Albelda and Marcos Senna in midfield and helped the team dominate all over the pitch. Cesc put in a solid display and, although he was substituted with twenty minutes left, had been on the field for both of Spain's goals.

Four days later, in Geneva, Fábregas came off the bench to spark his team to a 2-1 win over Croatia. It was only a brief fifteen-minute cameo, but he certainly breathed life into the side and Fernando Torres popped up with a late winner. Back-to-back wins improved morale and sent the Spaniards into the tournament in good form. Croatia had qualified for the World Cup, making this victory all the more praiseworthy. Question marks remained, though, over whether Aragones had decided on his starting line-up. Xabi Alonso and Xavi had started against the Croatians and some felt this was an indication that they were the manager's favoured midfield pairing. Fábregas just got his head down and worked hard in training – it was all he could do to impress Aragones.

Cesc was confident the Spanish side could achieve great things at the tournament. He told the media: 'It's true that we haven't really done well in previous World Cups, but now it is completely different. There are only three players who were in the last World Cup so we feel ready. We are playing well at the moment. The confidence is very high in the team and country, and I think we just have to keep going with the same mentality.'

It was significant that there were a number of new faces in the Spanish set-up. It limited the effect of the ghosts of previous failures. The 1998 and 2002 World Cups had not ended well for the Spanish, but this was a fresh group who were not hindered by those memories. They were starting with a clean slate. This was their chance to write themselves into the country's history books and put down a marker for future years.

Fábregas added: 'It is very difficult to get to the final,

but we have a great team with a great country and great manager. I'm sure we have all the right conditions to win the World Cup.'

It was a positive statement of intent but, as Fábregas acknowledged, there were plenty of other sides desperate to lift the Jules Rimet trophy. Holders Brazil looked strong, as did fellow South Americans Argentina. Other European sides also posed a threat, particularly Italy and the hosts, Germany. And then there was England, too – Cesc knew all about them and if Spain were not triumphant in the competition, England would surely be the midfielder's next choice.

It was a hot summer in Germany and the tournament attracted hordes of fans from all over the world. Spanish supporters travelled with optimism and shirt sales went through the roof, forcing extra production in the warehouses. They would make sure that Fábregas and his colleagues received loud backing in each game, acting as a twelfth man. There would be Spanish flags galore whenever the team played. And, of course, back home there was no end of hype as the start of the tournament neared.

It was incredible to think that Cesc had been a fifteen-year-old schoolboy in Barcelona during the previous World Cup in Japan and South Korea, still dreaming of a career as a professional footballer and watching the matches on television. Now he was heading to the tournament himself as one of the most highly rated youngsters in the world. The interceding four years had been a whirlwind adventure and he hoped that it would continue with a strong World Cup run.

There was no doubt the Spanish squad had an

embarrassment of riches in the middle of the field. Barcelona's Xavi and Liverpool's Xabi Alonso were just two of the central midfield players competing with Cesc for a place in the starting line-up. Fábregas acknowledged that he would have to fight hard for a spot in the side and put a positive spin on the situation, telling reporters: 'Everyone wants to be in the first XI so I think that is very important for the competition in the team.' Deep down, though, he was hopeful of breaking into Aragones' plans.

Spain had been drawn in Group H, along with Ukraine, Tunisia and Saudi Arabia and were expected to make the second round without any problems. Some experts felt the Spaniards could go all the way in Germany; others, including Paco Lloret of Canal Nou TV, were more sceptical. Lloret claimed: 'I'm not very confident about the national team. They are good players, but never can reach the semi-finals. I don't expect a successful World Cup.' Seemingly, experts were divided. Were the Spanish squad finally set to come good on their dark-horse tag or would it be a familiar story of underachievement?

Cesc found himself on the bench for Spain's tournament opener against Ukraine in Leipzig on 14 June. He was naturally disappointed but supported his colleagues whole-heartedly as Aragones opted for Xavi and Xabi Alonso in the central areas, with Marcos Senna also preferred to Fábregas. Ukraine's main threat would come from Andriy Shevchenko and Cesc knew that Spain could take nothing for granted against their skilful opponents. He had seen how deadly Shevchenko could be when given a sight of goal.

In the end, though, it turned out to be a rout as the Spaniards produced a clinical display to sweep aside the Ukrainians 4-0. The goals were shared around, with Alonso, Villa (2) and Torres on the scoresheet. Fábregas waited patiently for his chance and enjoyed the passion of the Spanish supporters as he warmed up. A red card for Ukraine defender Vladislav Vashchuk ended the game as a contest when the score was 2-0 and from then on Spain were untouchable. Cesc joined the action in the second half, sampling thirteen minutes on his World Cup debut and taking his place in his country's history books as their youngest-ever World Cup player. He was just 19 years and 41 days old. The match might have been decided by that stage, but Fábregas was typically energetic in midfield as the Ukrainians wilted. The game was not over for him and every moment on the pitch was an opportunity to prove his worth to the management.

After the game, the mood in the Spanish camp was hugely positive. The team had played with great style and many speculated on whether this team could erase all the heartache of previous tournaments. Ukraine were supposed to be their toughest group-stage opponents and the Spaniards had destroyed them. They had certainly made a bright start and looked the most impressive nation so far in the competition – certainly more eye-catching than the laborious Brazilians, who had edged past Croatia.

Thrilled to become Spain's youngest-ever World Cup performer and more optimistic than ever about the side's chances, Fábregas told *Marca* newspaper: 'I am very happy. For a player to make his World Cup debut is special, but now I want more and more.' He also showed the unity within the squad when he diplomatically answered questions about starting on the bench: 'We are a team. The manager is the one who decides because he wants to win and if he picks this team, it is because he thinks it is the best.'

Spanish boss Aragones admitted the start had been a very encouraging one, telling the press: 'If we show what we can do I know we can be among the top teams at this tournament. At first I thought it was going to be more complicated, but the second goal made Ukraine more crestfallen and the rest was easier.' But he refused to get carried away by the impressive margin of victory and would clearly be keeping the players' feet on the ground: 'We didn't expect such a good start, but we were lucky to score early goals from two set-pieces. We need to make a fair analysis of the game. We enjoyed all the luck.'

The other game in Spain's group – between Tunisia and Saudi Arabia – ended 2-2. The Spaniards sat proudly at the top of the group table and Cesc wasted no time in telling the media that the team had the perfect balance: 'Every team has their tricks: there are sides that are stronger, but less technically gifted or the reverse, but I believe that Spain has a very good mix.' Maybe this would be their tournament. Maybe the years of hurt would be put behind them. Maybe Fábregas would help to take the team all the way to the final. The answers would be revealed over the coming weeks as a seemingly endless stream of football hit television screens worldwide.

The World Cup was making a huge impact on Germany. The Germans were doing a superb job as hosts, the atmosphere around the country was electric and supporters were generally well behaved. Football was all anyone wanted to talk about and, with several matches each day during the group stages, there was plenty of action. Cesc was honoured to be representing his country and playing on the biggest stage of all.

On 19 June, Spain sought their second victory as they faced Tunisia in Stuttgart. Fábregas remained confident of his team's chances and hoped to get a longer opportunity to prove his worth on the pitch. As expected, the Spaniards were unchanged, meaning that Cesc was again named among the substitutes for the game. But he would have a key role to play in this match and would push himself into Aragones' plans.

The Spaniards made a nightmare start, falling behind after eight minutes, and never fully regained their composure in the first half. Fábregas could only watch in dismay as his colleagues failed to find any rhythm going forward against less talented opponents. Aragones was far from amused. With Spain trailing 1-0 at half-time, he made two changes. Luis Garcia was replaced by Raul and, most significantly, Marcos Senna made way for Fábregas. Cesc was determined to make the most of this chance and he, more than anyone, helped turn the match around for his side.

Gradually, Tunisia began to tire and Fábregas quickly stamped his authority on the game. Spain's equaliser came after seventy-two minutes. Cesc has never been shy to try his luck with long-range shots and it paid dividends on this occasion. His strike was fumbled by the Tunisian goalkeeper and Raul netted the rebound. Fábregas was not finished yet though. Four minutes later, his pinpoint pass behind the Tunisia defence released Torres, who comfortably made it 2-1. The game had been turned on its head. Torres added a third from the penalty spot late on, but there was no doubt who had been the catalyst for the win – Fábregas had been superb. His family were immensely proud and crossed their fingers that Spain would enjoy a lengthy run in the tournament. There would be more big parties in his home town if Fábregas kept this up.

Aragones knew his substitutions had been vital and made a note of the impact Cesc had made on proceedings. He was relieved to pick up the win, telling the media: 'I knew it would be a very complicated and difficult game. It was tremendously difficult to break through. After Cesc took a shot and Raul got the goal, it became much easier to open them up.' The Spanish boss added: 'Cesc interpreted his role very well. He directed the team to play our game.' Maybe the youngster would now get a starting role for Spain's final group game.

Fábregas also addressed the press: 'We played a big second half. We are on the right track, but we could improve some things. I went out onto the pitch to do what I always do – to play football and enjoy myself. We have shown that we are a winning team.'

The youngster was doing a good job of handling all the media attention. His name was cropping up in the voting process for the tournament's Best Young Player award. Though Ecuador's Luis Valencia and Portugal's Cristiano Ronaldo seemed the likeliest winners at this early stage, it was flattering for Cesc to be mentioned as a candidate for such an honour. Plus, there was still time for the Spaniard to stake his claim.

Fábregas' display had pleased all those who had seen it, including the great Argentine playmaker Diego Maradona, who told Spanish television station *Cuatro*: 'Cesc gave Spain the final ball it was lacking in the first half.' In a personal address to the Spaniard, Maradona added: 'I hope you carry on playing football like that. It was spectacular.' It could not get much better than this for Cesc.

The victory over Tunisia put Spain into the second round, taking the pressure off the players for their final group match against Saudi Arabia in Kaiserslautern on 23 June. Aragones took the chance to shuffle his pack a little and Fábregas was named in the starting line-up – a reward for his bright displays off the bench in the past two games. He could not wait to sample the feeling of walking out onto the pitch at a World Cup and lining up for the national anthems. However, even though Aragones had made numerous changes, there was still a sense of this being a meaningless match.

The Spaniards rather went through the motions in the afternoon heat, but did enough to seal a 1-0 win thanks to Gutierrez Juanito's header from a Reyes free-kick. Cesc was again prominent in midfield, offering clever link-up play and forcing a good save from Mabrouk Zaid in the Saudi Arabia goal. He was replaced for the final twenty five minutes, but felt happy with his performance, believing he had done enough to give Aragones a major selection headache ahead of the second round. The quality of Spain's play in the second half disappointed their manager, but it was hard to be too upset considering the team had taken maximum points from their three games, scoring eight goals and conceding just one. Thus far the players had avoided the pitfalls of previous tournaments.

Fábregas' displays during the group stage had clearly caught Aragones' attention. He was playing without fear and this allowed him to produce his best form. Despite all the media attention at the tournament and the intense atmosphere in the stadiums, he kept his head. He was still riding the crest of the Champions League wave and knew he had more than held his own in the starting line-up against Saudi Arabia. He was playing well beyond his years and his reputation was growing with every game.

France would be Spain's second-round opponents. Ahead of the clash, Cesc hoped to keep his place and Aragones granted this wish, selecting him ahead of Villarreal midfielder Senna. The manager wanted more creativity and felt that Cesc was the man for the moment. It ranked alongside the 2005 FA Cup final and the 2006 Champions League final as the biggest games of Fábregas' career to date. The Spaniards had not expected to face France in the second round. Most had predicted France would top their group, as Spain had done, but Switzerland had pipped the French to first place in Group G, setting up a mouth-watering second round clash between two of Europe's finest teams.

It was frustrating for Fábregas and company. The Spanish camp correctly viewed Switzerland as easier opponents, but would now have to outwit the likes of Vieira, Zidane and Henry to reach the quarter-finals. It would be intriguing to see the Spanish young guns like Fábregas and Torres facing the veterans in the French side. Cesc tried to keep his excitement under control as he prepared for one of the biggest games of his career. He and his team-mates carried the expectations of a nation. Writing for the *Independent*, Gerry Francis gave his verdict ahead of the match: 'For the last few championships I've had a bet on Spain. In Cesc Fábregas, they've got a player who's blossoming, is used to big games and can make the difference.'

But this would not be a memorable night for the Spaniards. Fábregas and his team-mates never really settled into their rhythm, but found themselves leading just before the half-hour mark as Lilian Thuram was adjudged to have fouled Pablo Ibanez in the penalty area. Villa converted the spot-kick and Cesc joined in the celebrations. Sadly, the joy was short-lived. Franck Ribery equalised before half-time and the French looked the superior side as Zidane rolled back the years with some vintage touches.

The second half struggled to separate the two sides. Cesc had some exciting moments without dominating the game as he had at times for Arsenal that season. The crucial moments came late on as Henry won a free-kick for a challenge by Barcelona defender Carlos Puyol, who was renewing his duel with the striker from the Champions League final, and the resulting delivery allowed Vieira to put France ahead. Just seven minutes remained. It was a crushing blow and left Fábregas and company little time to respond. They were shell-shocked as their world came crashing down around them.

As Spain pushed forward desperately for a dramatic equaliser, the French put the game to bed. Zidane capped an excellent individual display by scoring a composed third on the break. The dream was over. The referee's whistle confirmed the 3-1 defeat and the Spanish players hung their heads in dismay. A competition that had started so brightly had ended as miserably as so many previous tournaments had done. Cesc had not put in one of his best displays against the French and, unfortunately, there would now be plenty of time to go over it in his mind. Another grilling from their national press awaited the Spanish squad as they prepared to pack their bags for home. The Spain dressing room was silent after the game. There was nothing to say. Fábregas and company just sat disconsolately, taking in the events of the past two hours.

The devastation within the camp was summed up by Xabi Alonso in his blog: 'When you have been knocked out of a World Cup, you just go back to the hotel, pick up your things and leave as soon as possible. There is no point in hanging around in Germany. You just want to draw a line under it all and get out of there.' Cesc's feelings were similar. It was just as well that he did not have to stick around with all the hype and media attention surrounding the tournament – it would have simply rubbed salt into the wounds.

Fábregas told the Spanish press how the agony of the defeat had left him with 'a bad taste in his mouth'. He explained: 'Elimination is hard to take. We have had a good tournament and we are leaving much earlier than anticipated. We had many expectations and to be heading home early makes it a little difficult. The people have been phenomenal from the first day up until today and, although we have lost, they have come to support us.'

He had loved the atmosphere of the occasion, but was bitterly disappointed with the result. He had worked so hard to earn a first-team place and now his World Cup was over. His rollercoaster 2006 season would live long in the memory but, ultimately, he had finished it empty-handed, despite all the improvements he had made to his game. On the plus side, though, he had enhanced his reputation and had played in the biggest tournament in world football. It was easy to forget just how impressive this was. He was still only nineteen years of age.

The experience of appearing at such a massive football event was a huge benefit to his game. As he later recalled: 'The World Cup helped me a lot because it is an experience you never forget. The most important thing is the club because that is where you train every day and where you are coached. But the national team can help with experience and the type of game you play.'

Meanwhile, the World Cup continued apace and the Spanish players could do nothing but spectate. Having set their hearts on reaching the latter stages, it made painful viewing and there was a lot of frustration that they were not taking part in the action. There was, though, plenty of entertainment left on show as the tournament reached the quarter-final stage with most of the other leading nations still involved. Arsenal fans hoped Fábregas would now be cheering for England, who reached the quarter-finals with a narrow 1-0 win over Ecuador – only to lose to Portugal on penalties.

Spain's conquerors, France, used the momentum from beating Cesc and company to surprise holders Brazil in the quarter-finals before gaining another narrow win in the semi-finals over Cristiano Ronaldo's Portugal. So Zidane-inspired France made it to the final, where they faced Italy, who overcame hosts Germany in extra-time in the other semi-final. The final was a tense contest that will forever be remembered for Zidane's extra-time head-butt on Marco Materazzi. The Italians went on to lift the trophy after winning a penalty shootout.

While Fábregas was pleased that his friends in the French camp had enjoyed such a good run in the competition, it did little to ease the pain he felt following Spain's early elimination from the competition. He had really hoped to reach the latter stages in Germany. But the disappointment would be the perfect spur for Cesc going into the new Premiership season. As he explained to *Marca*: 'What I want now is to get myself into the best possible shape for the coming season.'

And of course, he was still young. There would be plenty more World Cups – and European Championships – ahead for Fábregas and the experience he had gained in Germany would undoubtedly help him become an even bigger hit at the next major tournament. As usual with Cesc, the disappointment left him frustrated but, once he had cooled off and come to terms with the defeat, he soon returned to his normal self. Life was too short to sulk for weeks on end. He now had new targets to aim for.

A key part of being a professional footballer is the ability to move on after setbacks. It is inevitable that there will be a handful of forgettable performances during any season – even the top players like Cesc cannot always produce their best form. The important part is the manner in which a footballer deals with these low points. It is easy to dwell on disappointments, but the ideal response is to put past fixtures to the one side, learn from them and focus on upcoming matches instead.

Cesc was already counting the days impatiently until

Euro 2008 in Austria and Switzerland. He would have two more Premiership seasons under his belt by then and would undoubtedly be one of Spain's leading lights at the tournament. However, despite forcing his way into the line-up during the World Cup, Fábregas' place in the national side was far from assured and the next twelve months of international football were a reminder that he could take nothing for granted in the Spanish set-up.

Cesc's performances in Germany had particularly caught the attention of Real Madrid and he jumped to the top of their transfer wishlist. It was easy to see why. With all the *galacticos* in the Madrid squad, a calm, measured passer would help to get the best out of the likes of Raul and Ronaldo. Reports flew in from all directions, claiming to know the latest on the situation.

In late June, Ramón Calderón, a candidate in the Real Madrid presidential elections, had claimed that he had agreed a deal to bring Fábregas to the Bernabeu if he was elected. It was suggested that Cesc's agent had accepted the terms of a five-year contract. The player himself said little about the matter, leading most to assume that it was merely wishful thinking on the part of Calderón. But the matter rumbled on.

It was a worrying time for Arsenal fans as reports maintained that the Spaniard would be leaving the club. Pedja Mijatovic, the Sporting Director of Calderón's campaign, told the media that 'Cesc and Kaka [of AC Milan] will play for Real Madrid' and it did plenty to unsettle Wenger as the Frenchman planned for the new season. Not knowing for certain whether Fábregas would be staying or going was a major concern, even if the Spaniard appeared to be committed to the club.

But Cesc was happy at Arsenal and had come so far in such a short space of time. He was becoming an increasingly influential figure in the first team and he would not find a better set-up anywhere in Europe. He was certain of that.

Playing in the World Cup in Germany had been a tremendous experience for Fábregas, but he wanted to keep looking forward. There was so much more he wanted to achieve and he had returned to Arsenal with an enhanced reputation after his performances at the tournament. Back in London to prepare for the new Premiership season, there was plenty going on at the club.

After all the emotions of saying farewell to Highbury, there was equal excitement about the move to the Emirates Stadium. Fábregas had enjoyed many special moments at Highbury, but he resolved to put them in the past and focus on the club's exciting future in their new home. The increased capacity – from 38,000 to 60,000 – meant that the atmosphere inside the stadium would be incredible and Cesc was excited to feel the intense support on match days. He told *Arsenal TV Online*: 'I think it [the Emirates Stadium] is fantastic. Everyone had great feelings about the stadium. We all hope we will win a lot of trophies here.'

Following the speculation over the summer, Fábregas was keen to give Arsenal fans the assurances they were desperate to hear, announcing to the media: 'Yes, I will definitely be staying. Real Madrid is a big club with a big history, but I am an Arsenal player. I always wanted to play for Arsenal and it is the club that has believed in me since I was sixteen years old. It's not easy for me to leave and I have to pay Arsène Wenger back for all he has done for me.'

Above: Fábregas takes the silver cup for Spain Under 17s, beaten 1-0 by Brazil in the 2003 World Championship.

Left: A jubilant Fábregas celebrates scoring the fifth goal against Wolverhampton Wanderers in the fourth round of the 2003 Carling Cup.

Expectations are high for the fresh-faced Fábregas, here shown at a press conference on the eve of Arsenal's Champions League match against Real Madrid.

Left: Bergkamp chases Fábregas during a practice session at the club's training ground in North London.

Below: Fábregas battles for the ball with Barcelona's Mark van Bommel during the UEFA Champions League final in May 2006.

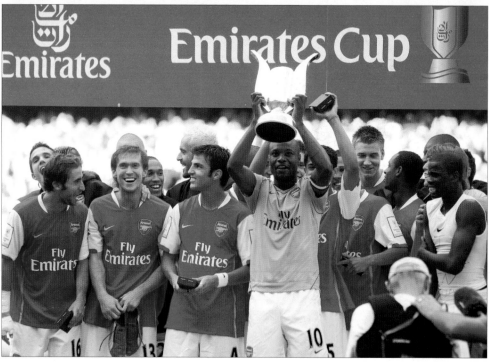

Above: Fábregas vies with Vieira as Spain play France in the 2006 World Cup.

Below: Arsenal celebrate their 2007 triumph over Inter Milan, lifting the Emirates trophy high in the air.

Fábregas
signing.

Above: Banter at an international training session in autumn 2007.

Below: Fábregas scores a stunning opener against AC Milan in the Champions League 2008.

Fábregas gets a pep talk from Wenger during training.

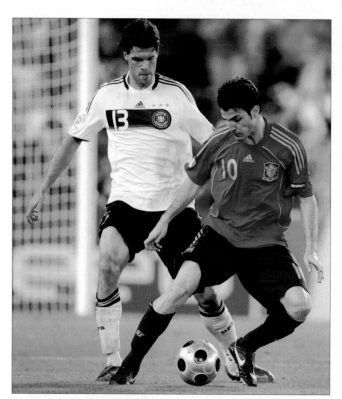

Left: Fábregas takes control during the Euro 2008 final.

Below: Keeping the ball away from Roy Keane in August 2004.

The other big news was that Henry was staying at Arsenal. The announcement came as a great boost to both the players and to Gunners fans. On several occasions, Henry had seemed destined to join Barcelona, but the lure of captaining Arsenal in their new stadium and staying with Wenger proved too hard to turn down. With the Frenchman onboard, Cesc knew the team had a far more intimidating look. The signing of creative midfielder Tomas Rosicky from Borussia Dortmund also appeared to be a useful piece of business and the Czech had shown glimpses of his talent with a couple of fine goals at the World Cup.

Cesc signalled the new era at the club by changing his shirt number from fifteen to four – the number formerly worn by Patrick Vieira. Far from being afraid of comparisons with the great Frenchman, he was eager to fill that role and it allowed him to emulate his hero Guardiola, who had worn the number four for Barcelona during Fábregas' childhood.

On a sadder note, Cesc had to say goodbye to a couple of popular faces during the summer months. Defender Sol Campbell, an integral part of the Invincibles team, opted to leave the club and pursue a fresh challenge at Portsmouth under Harry Redknapp. Likewise, Robert Pires sought pastures new after Arsenal only offered him a one-year extension to his contract. He joined Spanish side Villarreal in a two-year deal. Both players had been great team-mates and would be missed. Pires, whose mother is Spanish, had been a massive help to Fábregas in the early days, speaking to him in his mother tongue and helping Cesc to settle.

Just to add to the drama, Wenger too was rumoured to

be leaving Arsenal as Real Madrid sources claimed that a deal was being done. An associate of Villar Mir, a candidate in the club's elections, revealed that discussions had taken place: 'For some reason, the subject has not been leaked until now. Wenger has a clause in his contract that allows him to leave if a sufficient offer comes in from Real and if Villar Mir is elected Wenger will be the next coach.' With the futures of Arsène and Henry up in the air, it had been a difficult summer. Now, though, both were staying and the Gunners could focus on reclaiming the Premiership title.

Elsewhere, Arsenal's fellow title challengers looked hungry. Chelsea's two-year league domination showed no signs of ending, especially with the additions of German midfielder Michael Ballack and Ukrainian front man Andriy Shevchenko. The arrival of Shevchenko cast doubts over the future of Didier Drogba. Clearly, Jose Mourinho had no end of options. Having spent around £30 million on Shevchenko, Chelsea looked set to use him as their focal point in attack.

By contrast, Manchester United had been fairly restrained. Michael Carrick was their only major purchase, costing £18.6 million, but Sir Alex Ferguson was delighted to welcome Paul Scholes back from a troublesome eye injury. Scholes is one of the players Fábregas looks up to most in the English game and he was pleased to hear of the United midfielder's recovery. He welcomed the competition.

Liverpool had also rebuilt over the summer in a desperate attempt to bring the title back to Merseyside. Fábregas knew it would be a tough ask for the Gunners to fight off such strong competition, but he remained confident about the team's ability.

The big question was whether the Arsenal side could improve their results away from home and find consistency on their travels. Too often over the last year, Cesc and his team-mates had been outfought in physical contests away from Highbury, particularly at places like Bolton and Blackburn. Pundits talked about the Gunners' inability to play their passing football against 'in your face' teams who closed down space and were strong in the tackle. Fábregas hated to see opponents employing long-ball tactics, but had to admit that it was proving the team's undoing. Could the squad put last season's woes on the road behind them?

As well as vowing to help improve the team's away form, Cesc also set himself the target of reaching a double-figure goal tally. The Spaniard discussed the topic with the media: 'A lot of people said to me last year that I should shoot more. I scored a lot of goals when I was young, but when you are young it is much easier. The last time I scored two goals in a game was three years ago in the reserves. If I can get ten [for the season] I will be happy. As I always say, though, for me setting up a goal is better than scoring.' This partly explained why he was not on the scoresheet so often.

Before the Arsenal squad could focus on their league campaign, they had a Champions League qualifier against Dinamo Zagreb to negotiate. Fábregas saw little to concern him in the Zagreb side but, with a place in Europe's premier club competition at stake, he refused to become complacent. In the first leg, in Croatia on 8 August, Cesc was the star of the show. Arsenal had failed to break through in the opening period, but Fábregas came to life in the final half hour, opening the scoring with a well-placed

119

shot. Van Persie doubled the lead a minute later before Cesc found the net again, outwitting several defenders and giving the Gunners a comfortable three-goal cushion for the return leg. If Fábregas could keep up this goalscoring form, Arsenal fans would be in for a special season and his ten-goal target would be achieved in no time.

An international friendly with Iceland came at the wrong time for Cesc as he tried to focus on club football. It was a bizarre idea to schedule a match so close to the start of some of the European leagues. He played sixty-eight minutes in a fairly dull 0-0 draw with neither team willing to over-exert themselves and it showed why such timetabling was not in the best interests of the game. Still, it was good match practice for Fábregas with the Premiership kick-off just days away in England.

Unfortunately, Arsenal's league campaign began in rocky fashion. All the hype surrounding the first league game at the Emirates seemed to distract the Gunners. Meanwhile, their opponents, Aston Villa, appeared to relish their role as party poopers in front of a crowd of 60,023. Arsenal needed a late equaliser from Gilberto Silva to rescue a point after Olof Mellberg had headed the visitors in front. It was not the start to the Emirates era Fábregas had dreamt of.

The atmosphere in the stadium at the final whistle was rather flat and the players were disappointed in the dressing room, having desperately wanted to put on a good show for the fans. While there was some mention of a new-ground jinx, Fábregas knew the Gunners simply had not been good enough on the day and that they had let down the Arsenal supporters who had poured into the ground, full of excitement.

An opportunity quickly arrived for the team to make amends. In midweek, the Gunners completed a 5-1 aggregate victory over Dinamo Zagreb and booked their place in the Champions League group stage. It was a big relief to everyone at the club. Fábregas and company did not play particularly well, but won 2-1 on the night. Incidentally, the Zagreb goal was scored by Eduardo Da Silva – a player who would make his way to Arsenal the following summer. Having reached the final of the competition last season, Cesc was eager to start another long European run. But this time, he wanted to lift the trophy.

Back in the Premiership, the Gunners' wobble continued away to Manchester City on 26 August. They were finding goals hard to come by, despite creating a hatful of chances. Arsenal dominated the first half at Eastlands yet trailed City at the interval. The Gunners found the path to goal blocked throughout the second period and returned to London nursing a 1-0 defeat. Cesc had not played badly, but Wenger wanted to see the Spaniard getting into goalscoring positions more often. Others needed to take more responsibility to relieve the burden on Henry's shoulders and stop the team becoming predictable.

Arsenal finally brought an end to the on-running Ashley Cole saga as they narrowly beat the transfer deadline to secure a swap deal that brought French defender William Gallas to the Emirates. The Gunners also received £5 million in the terms of the deal. Cole had been unhappy at the club for months and it made sense for Wenger to offload him, especially when a player of Gallas' calibre became available. Fábregas and Cole had never been close, as the defender revealed in his autobiography. Though Cesc rated the left-back as a footballer, he knew Gael Clichy was waiting in the wings and could fill Cole's spot in the side. Plus, Fábregas was excited at the possibility of a Gallas-Toure partnership in central defence that would rank alongside the best in Europe. All in all, it looked as though Wenger had pulled off another coup.

It was yet another example of the Arsenal manager's ability to bring in top players without spending huge sums of money. The Frenchman had balanced the books so effectively during his time in charge of the North London club. Thanks to the Frenchman's eye for talent and his faith in young players, the Gunners were in a strong financial position. Who else could have tempted Cesc away from Barcelona or picked up Kolo Toure for a mere £150,000? Such is Wenger's perfect understanding of the economic side of football that the following year he would make it clear to billionaire Alisher Usmanov, who was reportedly working on a takeover bid, that he did not need extra funds for transfers. As Fábregas knew, Arsène had that aspect under control.

Cesc headed back to his homeland for the international break as Spain began their qualifying campaign for Euro 2008. Drawn in Group F, they would face Liechtenstein, Denmark, Sweden, Latvia, Iceland and Northern Ireland. They kicked off on 2 September against Liechtenstein in Badajoz, winning 4-0. Fábregas, off the back of his excellent World Cup form, was picked in the starting line-up and played sixty-three minutes before he was replaced by Iniesta. By this time Spain were 3-0 up and cruising to victory.

Four days later away to Northern Ireland, things were not quite so rosy – far from it, in fact. Cesc started on the bench, but was soon sent into the action after David Albelda limped off through injury. This, though, was a humbling night for the Spanish as a David Healy hat-trick condemned the visitors to a 3-2 defeat. Fábregas could not believe it. Maybe they had underestimated their opponents.

He was still stunned by the result when he arrived back in North London. Sadly, the international break did little to improve Arsenal's fortunes in the Premiership. A second home league fixture brought a second home draw as frustration mounted at the Emirates against Middlesbrough. The Gunners needed an Henry penalty to rescue a 1-1 draw from a match they had expected to win. Fábregas was in the thick of the action, forcing Boro goalkeeper Mark Schwarzer into a couple of good saves. Manchester United had collected twelve points out of twelve and sat top of the Premiership; Arsenal had two points from their three games. Cesc knew the Gunners were making life tough for themselves. Performances had to improve quickly, because a slow start could prove terminal for their title hopes. As Fábregas acknowledged, when Arsenal went a goal behind at home, they always faced an uphill battle. The first goal in these games was so crucial.

Arsenal got back to winning ways with a 2-1 victory in Europe over Hamburg. Having been drawn in Group G, Fábregas and company would also face Jose Mourinho's former club Porto and CSKA Moscow. The three points in Germany were a welcome boost, especially considering the absence of the injured Henry. Cesc once again played the full ninety minutes and was relieved the team would be in the headlines for the right reasons this time.

The win also improved morale ahead of the trip to Old Trafford on 17 September to face the league leaders, Manchester United. With Chelsea leaving both clubs trailing during the previous season, Arsenal and United had a point to prove. So far, it was Sir Alex Ferguson's side that had made the big statements, but Fábregas knew that a victory in United's backyard would put the Gunners back in the title race. It promised to be a tense afternoon for all involved.

Cesc had taken part in some fiery clashes with United in past years. The 'Battle of the Buffet' in 2004 would live long in the memory, as would the tunnel fracas in 2005. Both games had ended in losses for Arsenal. It had not taken Fábregas long to understand the intensity of the rivalry between the two clubs and he was desperate to put one over on Sir Alex's side. The Momentum was certainly with United's, though, as they sought to protect their 100 per cent start to the season. Arsenal, meanwhile, were looking for their first league win.

It was an eventful contest, in which Arsenal kept the United big guns quiet. Rooney contributed little up front for the home side, while Ronaldo struggled to make his usual impact. The Gunners won a first-half penalty when Tomas Kuszczak, deputising for Edwin van der Sar, fouled Emmanuel Adebayor. Gilberto Silva stepped up to the spot but, to Fábregas' dismay, Kuszczak guessed right and saved well. It was a let-off for United; Arsenal had to be more ruthless.

But another chance would come. As United became increasingly frustrated, Cesc drove his side forward. With just four minutes remaining, the Gunners found the knockout blow, thanks largely to Fábregas' vision. The youngster chased and harried Ronaldo into a mistake in his own half and seized on the loose ball. Cesc dribbled goalwards before sliding a clever ball through to Adebayor, who placed the ball under Kuszczak and into the net. The away end of the ground went wild; the Arsenal players celebrated a priceless goal. Wenger was ecstatic as the Gunners held on for the victory and the Frenchman chatted excitedly with Fábregas as they headed down the tunnel. The Spaniard had made the match-winning contribution.

Wenger was delighted with Cesc and the rest of the side, telling the press: 'A loss could have been decisive, but this win reinforces the belief that we are a very strong side. We controlled the game and always looked good technically. Everyone in the team played well, gave everything and showed quality.' Nobody had shown more quality than Fábregas and United captain Gary Neville paid the Spaniard an indirect compliment by saying: 'When you make mistakes in midfield, they [Arsenal] are as good as anybody in making you pay.'

Having beaten United without Henry, confidence was high again around the Emirates. The Frenchman returned to the side for the visit of Sheffield United on 23 September and the Gunners completed a 3-0 victory, with all the goals coming in the final twenty-five minutes. Despite suffering a cut lip during the game, Fábregas produced some sublime moments, including the assist for Gallas to give Arsenal the lead. It was a more comfortable home game than had been the case against

Aston Villa and Middlesbrough. The jinx had been lifted; the Gunners had won in the league at home.

A midweek clash with Porto saw the Gunners keep another clean sheet on the way to a solid 2-0 victory. Henry and Hleb scored the goals while Fábregas twice went close to getting on the scoresheet. Maximum points so far in Europe represented an excellent start. Arsenal grabbed a fifth-consecutive win at the weekend away at Charlton, coming from behind to win 2-1. Van Persie grabbed both goals and his second was a phenomenal volley from the edge of the penalty area. Again, Cesc found himself in good positions and twice forced good stops from Charlton goalkeeper Scott Carson. But the goals just would not come for him.

The international break saw Fábregas meeting up with his international colleagues for two fixtures – firstly a Euro 2008 qualifier against Sweden and then a friendly with Argentina. After the defeat to Northern Ireland in their last qualifier, the Spaniards needed a positive response against the Swedes to stamp their authority on the group. Cesc received another starting role as Aragones continued to show faith in the youngster's eye for a pass.

This, though, was a game to forget for Fábregas – on a personal and team level. Sweden won 2-0 and dominated the contest, scoring in the first and last ten minutes. It made it two losses from three games, three points out of a possible nine for Spain – this was not good enough. After making heavy weather of their World Cup qualifying group, the Spanish squad had not learned their lessons. Cesc knew he and his team-mates faced an uphill battle to claim top spot now and feared that his own below-par display might cost him his place in the starting line-up.

It was always nice to catch up with the likes of Xavi on these trips, but the mood was negative after the loss to Sweden. Cesc was named among the substitutes for the friendly with Argentina and only entered the action for the final fifteen minutes. David Villa's second-half penalty proved decisive as Spain claimed an impressive 2-1 win that gave the morale in the camp a little boost, even if the result did not count for any points. It might have only been a friendly but matches like these were vital for establishing team spirit and giving Aragones the chance to test out his favoured line-ups.

Back in domestic action, the Gunners' run of victories stretched to six against Watford at the Emirates on 14 October. Henry was in terrific form, as was Fábregas, who was involved in all of Arsenal's best moments. Premiership newcomers Watford had little answer to the passing and movement of the Gunners' line-up and their pace frightened the life out of the visitors' defence. Cesc and his colleagues were putting their slow start behind them and were moving up the table. This was the type of home display the Arsenal supporters had expected on a regular basis; their side were far more clinical and incisive than in the draws with Aston Villa and Middlesbrough.

A defeat away to CSKA Moscow in the Champions League ended Arsenal's hot streak. In the freezing temperatures of the Russian capital, the Gunners succumbed 1-0 against skilful opponents and surrendered their 100 percent record in Group G. Coping with the weather conditions and the state of the pitch were new experiences for Fábregas, but he acquitted himself well in midfield. Nonetheless, he was disappointed with the defeat, especially considering the referee appeared to have wrongly ruled out a late equaliser from Henry for an alleged handball.

Qualification, though, still appeared comfortable for Arsenal and Wenger shrugged off the loss post-match and joined Henry in criticising the referee: 'The referee has not seen anything, I felt it was a goal. We have to accept sometimes that referees give goals because they do not see things. Now we have something new – they cancel goals because they saw things which do not exist. That's a problem.'

Mid-October brought better news for Fábregas as he signed a new eight-year contract at the club, keeping him at Arsenal until 2014. Cesc wasted no time in expressing his delight at agreeing terms, telling the Arsenal club website: 'I am so happy here. I wanted to pay back the club, especially Arsène Wenger for the support and faith he has shown in me. What is important now is for the team to realise its potential and win trophies. That is our main aim, that is my aim as well.' The future at the club excited him greatly.

The frustrations of losing in Moscow in the Champions League were carried into the Gunners' clash with Reading as they cut through the Royals with an emphatic display of attacking football. Henry scored in the opening minute, after a magical run by Fábregas, and it was all Arsenal from then on as they cruised to a 4-0 win. Cesc was also involved in the fourth goal. He was bundled over in the penalty area as he prepared to shoot and Henry scored from the spot. Fábregas was then given the night off in midweek as a young Gunners side beat West Brom in the Carling Cup. The club were on a roll domestically.

The next month, though, was bitterly disappointing for Arsenal as their hopes of Premiership glory began to fade fast. The team dropped silly points and became rattled too easily on their travels. The rot began with a 1-1 draw at home to Everton. The Toffees took the lead early and it was a familiar story at the Emirates as the Gunners poured forward to try to rescue something from the game. Van Persie equalised, but the winning goal failed to materialise, despite good efforts from Fábregas and Henry. The team's scoring woes continued in midweek as they collected a 0-0 draw at the Emirates against CSKA Moscow. Teams seemed to have found the answer to stopping Arsenal.

On 5 November, the Gunners travelled to face West Ham at Upton Park for one of their many London derbies that season. Needing a win to boost morale, Arsenal fell to a late Marlon Harewood goal as Wenger and Hammers boss Alan Pardew seemed to square up on the touchline. It was an utterly forgettable day. Cesc and company had chances earlier on, but ultimately paid the price for squandering them. Fábregas was all too aware that the team had scored just one goal in their last three games – that simply was not good enough for a side wanting to mount a title challenge.

Cesc was becoming increasingly frustrated with the way his team-mates were being criticised by the media and with the fact that everyone was so keen to draw direct comparisons with the past. Fábregas had made his feelings clear on several occasions, including during an interview with the *Independent*: 'You cannot say, "Oh,

Diaby the new Vieira, [Emmanuel] Adebayor the new Kanu, Theo Walcott the new Henry." Maybe they will [be] in the future, but you cannot tell them now they will be the next guys.'

The Arsenal youngsters grabbed another good Carling Cup win in midweek before the first team followed suit at the weekend against Liverpool. It was a mystery to Fábregas why the Gunners raised their game against the top sides yet fell short against some of the league's weaker teams. Flamini, Toure and Gallas grabbed the goals as Arsenal picked up a valuable win. Cesc was involved in all three goals. His contribution for the opener was particularly important as he surged into the area and cut the ball back for Flamini to score from close range. This was much more like it.

Wenger praised his players after the game and hoped the victory could kick-start a title surge: 'Everybody played well; the players with big responsibilities were all strong for us. Liverpool played well, but the first goal was very important. We want to fight for the championship, so need to beat the big teams at home.' This was something Arsène had always felt was critical.

Fábregas had to jet off to Spain in midweek for an international friendly against Romania. It was another low-key affair with the players focused on their club commitments and Romania edged a disappointing contest 1-0. Cesc played the first half, but was withdrawn at the interval as Aragones rung the changes to avoid the wrath of club managers. It came as somewhat of a relief that this was Spain's final friendly of 2006. Much as Fábregas enjoyed representing his country, fitting international fixtures around the domestic calendar was not ideal and he usually had to travel further than the rest of his Spanish team-mates.

Back in London, however, the visit of Newcastle the following weekend brought another frustrating draw. Yet again, a visiting team came to the Emirates and took the lead as Kieron Dyer found the net on the half-hour mark. Henry equalised with twenty minutes to go, but the Gunners failed to find the winning goal, as Fábregas had several chances but failed to make the most of them. Once more, the home fans were filled with disappointment as they left the stadium at the final whistle. The mood was improved in midweek, though, as Arsenal beat Hamburg 3-1 in the Champions League to go top of Group G, with Cesc creating countless openings for his team-mates. At least things were falling into place in Europe.

Then came two soul-destroying defeats in the space of four days as the Gunners' season hit the rocks, leaving Fábregas distraught. It had looked as though Arsenal were back on track, yet their away-day woes came back to haunt them. First, they were soundly beaten 3-1 by Bolton at the Reebok Stadium on 25 November, with former Gunner Nicolas Anelka doing the damage, scoring twice. Bolton had yet again found a way to beat the Gunners. Arsenal had produced a below–par performance, though, and Fábregas left the field angered that the home side's midfield had limited his impact. They were now twelve points behind the leaders Manchester United and the young Spaniard felt the title slipping further and further away.

A 2-1 defeat away to Fulham on 29 November made matters even worse. Wenger decided that Fábregas needed a rest after featuring so often throughout the season, but probably regretted the decision after the first twenty minutes, by which time Fulham were 2-0 ahead. Van Persie pulled a goal back before half-time and then Cesc was sent on to try to rescue something from the match. Unfortunately, despite the improved creativity Fábregas brought to the line-up, the Gunners could not claw themselves back into the match. Senderos was red-carded in the sixty-sixth minute and the home side clung on stubbornly for the three points. It had been a wretched week for Cesc and his team-mates.

Unsurprisingly, Wenger looked irritated after the game. His team had performed well, particularly in the second half, but the luck had been against them. The Frenchman told the media: 'I can't fault the team, but it's difficult when you're 2-0 down early on. Of course we are down and disappointed, but it's part of your job to cope with that – if you want to play at the top level, sometimes it doesn't go your way.' It was a lesson Fábregas was beginning to learn. The season was only just entering the month of December and Arsenal were floundering.

With Henry facing a spell on the sidelines, the North London derby against Tottenham could not have come at a worse time. Cesc, though, remained upbeat and the side put in their best performance for several weeks, with Adebayor opening the scoring and Gilberto with two penalties, one in each half, sealing a 3-0 victory. Fábregas again pushed forward into good positions, but the goals just would not come for him. Still, a win over Spurs was always a cause for a celebration and it gave the Arsenal fans bragging rights over their North London neighbours yet again.

The games kept coming thick and fast. The Gunners travelled to Portugal in midweek for an important tie with Porto. Despite all the minutes Fábregas had played in recent weeks, he was included in the starting line-up and fought hard to secure a 0-0 draw that put Arsenal into the second round. Cesc was excited by the prospect of another long run in the Champions League. It may have been an exhausting and generally disheartening few weeks, but the squad had to rouse themselves again as they faced Chelsea at Stamford Bridge on 10 December.

Though the Gunners were off the pace in the Premiership, Fábregas and his team-mates were desperate to put a dent in the Blues' title bid. Normally, this would have been a clash between two sides chasing the trophy, but Arsenal's poor start to the season meant that United and Chelsea held a comfortable advantage over them in the league. Nonetheless, Cesc was fired up and was desperate to put in a good performance. There was still nothing to compare to the atmosphere inside the stadiums during these types of matches and it inspired him to put on a good show.

It proved to be a compelling contest. The travelling Gunners fans predictably jeered Ashley Cole at every opportunity and their team matched the Blues stride for stride. There were a few scares, though, as Fábregas had to make a goal-line clearance in the first half to keep the game goalless. Chelsea became increasingly frustrated as the Gunners harried, chased and forced the champions into mistakes. After some comedy theatrics from Jens Lehmann and Didier Drogba, Arsenal grew in confidence and shocked Stamford Bridge by taking the lead with just

133

twelve minutes to go. Flamini played a neat one-two with Hleb and his shot beat Petr Cech. 1-0.

To Fábregas' dismay, the Blues fought back and equalised through a stunning Michael Essien strike. It was the only way Chelsea were going to get past the Arsenal rearguard – a sensational hit with the outside of the boot. Cesc dug in late on to protect the 1-1 scoreline and the Gunners could feel very pleased with their afternoon's work. They had certainly done United a favour. Fábregas had gone toe-to-toe with Frank Lampard in midfield and had not given an inch.

Wenger, though, was disappointed: 'I feel a bit frustrated because before the goal they [Chelsea] scored looked to be a foul on Alexander Hleb. We were in control, there was not much time left and we could have scored a second on the counter attack.' Ever the perfectionist, Arsène had wanted to cut the gap between his team and Chelsea. Fábregas took plenty of positives from the performance and a number of experts agreed with Wenger that Arsenal had probably deserved more than a point that afternoon.

Buoyed by their solid display at Stamford Bridge, the Gunners collected three points from their trip to face Wigan, but needed a late Adebayor goal to sneak a 1-0 win. Wenger finally gave Cesc another rest, leaving the Spaniard on the bench – a wise move considering the exertions of the past weeks. In Fábregas' absence, though, Arsenal struggled to break through and Wigan held their own for much of the game.

Fearing more dropped points, Wenger sent Cesc and van Persie into the action with fifteen minutes to go and it paid dividends as the side instantly looked livelier.

Tiring Wigan legs were exploited as Fábregas played a pinpoint pass over the home side's back four and Adebayor did the rest. It just showed how important Cesc was to this Gunners side. Arsène would be even more reluctant to rest the youngster now. The long trip back was a lot happier than it might have been but for Fábregas' contribution off the bench.

For all the improvements Arsenal had shown in away games, the team continued to drop points at the Emirates. It was a reversal of the previous campaign when their struggles came on the road. The latest visiting side to leave with a share of the spoils was Portsmouth, who gained a 2-2 draw and might have had more after going 2-0 up. The Gunners' comeback had been impressive, but they were seemingly forever playing catch-up in home games. Fábregas forced Pompey keeper David James into one good save and was a driving force as Arsenal clawed their way back to parity.

A week later, on 23 December, the Gunners finally hit top form at the Emirates, hammering Blackburn 6-2. It was a masterclass in attacking football and, although three goals in the final five minutes gave the scoreline a flattering look, Wenger was delighted with his forwards. Van Persie scored twice and the other goals were shared between Gilberto, Hleb, Adebayor and Flamini. However, although glossed over on the day, the fact they had conceded two goals once again at home would need addressing. Fábregas thoroughly enjoyed the occasion – his only disappointment was his failure to find the net in the rout. He had numerous opportunities to score but just was not clinical enough and luck seemed to be against him. The bottom line, however, was that Cesc had not scored for Arsenal since August.

Wenger was thrilled with the quality of football his team had produced, yet also found time to praise Blackburn's positive approach. He told the media after the game: 'Many teams have got away with a point playing less football than Blackburn have and they came here and played.' Rovers' style of play would be a hot topic for Cesc later in the season.

The Christmas period was bringing out the best in the Gunners. A 2-1 win at Watford on Boxing Day kept the momentum going, with van Persie scoring the winner with seven minutes left. Fábregas looked a little weary at times, but sparked into life as the team chased the decisive goal. The three points saw Arsenal move into third place, handing them an advantage over Liverpool, Bolton and Portsmouth, who were all fighting with the Gunners for a Champions League berth.

But a trip to Sheffield United on 30 December was a reminder of the flaws in the Arsenal squad as they were out-muscled by the Premiership newcomers and lost 1-0. Fábregas and his team-mates were still susceptible to aggressive marking and the home side did not give the visitors any time in possession. Cesc began the match on the bench as Wenger opted to ring the changes – a move that backfired badly. Fábregas was introduced after sixty-four minutes, but the damage had been done and even the Spaniard could not turn things around, despite midfielder Phil Jagielka being called into emergency service in goal for the Blades. It was an embarrassing evening, especially considering that Neil Warnock had also fielded several fringe players for a match he did not expect to win.

Wenger let it be known that such performances were unacceptable. It was a long journey back to London and it gave the players plenty of time to think about the defeat. Fábregas was only too aware that title-winning sides had to be able to cope with tricky away fixtures. The Gunners had not done so this season. But there was still plenty to play for: Cesc and his team-mates were still involved in the FA Cup, Carling Cup and Champions League.

CHAPTER 5
PLAYING CATCH-UP

Entering the New Year, Cesc knew the Gunners had to make amends for their poor start to the season and hoped to spark a fightback.

Fábregas and his team-mates began 2007 in style with a 4-0 home win over Charlton. Van Persie scored twice and Arsenal were sparked by the return to fitness of Thierry Henry. Cesc's link-up play was typically precise and his shot led to the penalty that saw Charlton defender Osei Sankofa sent off after just twenty-nine minutes. Henry opened the scoring from the spot. Special mention should also go to Justin Hoyte, who grabbed the team's second goal. As Jim van Wijk of *PA Sport* observed, it was the first time since September 2005 that an English player in an Arsenal shirt had found the net in the Premiership – an incredible statistic! However, considering that Wenger's stance had allowed the likes of Fábregas to emerge from the youth system, it was hard to scoff at the manager's reluctance to field English players.

Why should he feel obliged to worry about whether he was damaging the state of the English game? It was an issue that would rumble on as England made stuttering progress in their Euro 2008 qualifying group.

Wenger had made one significant move during the January transfer window, completing a loan deal that sent Jose Antonio Reyes to Real Madrid until the end of the season in exchange for Brazilian Julio Baptista. Baptista had been prolific at Sevilla, but had failed to make an impact in Madrid among the posse of *galacticos*. His ability, though, was unquestionable and he could play in midfield or up front. No doubt the Brazilian would be eager to get on the end of Cesc's pinpoint passing. It was a front-man's dream to play alongside someone who could spot runs so early and deliver the perfect ball. With youngster Theo Walcott, signed from Southampton in 2006, not yet deemed ready for regular first-team outings, Arsène had moved quickly to bring in another forward to give himself more options.

Suspension kept Fábregas out of the FA Cup third-round clash with Liverpool at Anfield. For once, though, he was not sorely missed as others stepped up to take on extra responsibility. Tomas Rosicky had one of his most influential games since signing in the summer, scoring two fine goals to leave the home side a mountain to climb. Cesc was ecstatic to see the team cruising to victory. Dirk Kuyt pulled a goal back in the second half, but Henry sealed a 3-1 victory with six minutes remaining with a stunning turn of pace. Fábregas looked forward to getting back into FA Cup action in the fourth round.

The two teams met again in midweek, this time in the

Carling Cup quarter-final. Both managers opted to select a blend of first-team stars, fringe players and youngsters, but it was Wenger's team that produced the vastly superior performance. Fábregas was one of the big names Arsène picked in the side and, along with fellow regulars Toure and Adebayor, he gave a flawless display. New boy Julio Baptista was the hero, bagging four goals and showing his true quality. It was a thrilling contest which ended 6-3 and there could have been even more goals – Baptista missed a penalty. It had been an excellent week for the Gunners and Cesc was delighted to see the team making such good progress. Two comprehensive victories over Liverpool were great for morale – now Arsenal had to kick on.

The run continued as January turned out to be the best month so far for Wenger's squad. There seemed to be a greater spirit in the side, reminiscent of that displayed during the previous season's Champions League run, and Blackburn were the next team to pay the price on 13 January. Arsenal won 2-0 at Ewood Park, despite having Gilberto sent off after just thirteen minutes. Kolo Toure gave ten-man Arsenal the lead and then Cesc helped set up the second, which Henry buried from long range. It was the type of match the Gunners had been losing or drawing earlier in the campaign; now they seemed to have the bit between their teeth. What better preparation for the visit of league leaders Manchester United?

Fábregas was desperate to put on a good show for United's first visit to the Emirates. Unsurprisingly, the stadium was packed and the crowd had come in the hope of seeing an Arsenal win. Cesc had great respect for the way Ferguson's side had been playing, but wanted nothing more than to sabotage their title bid. It was a big weekend of Premiership football. Earlier in the day, a depleted Chelsea side had travelled to Anfield and lost 2-0 to Liverpool, giving United a major boost and the chance to extend their advantage at the top of the table to nine points.

As always seems to be the case when Ferguson and Wenger go head to head, it was a close, tense match. Cesc found life tough in midfield in the first half as Paul Scholes and Michael Carrick dominated possession, stopping the Spaniard from having his usual influence on proceedings. Ferguson was clearly wary of Fábregas' ability to drive the Gunners forward. The game remained goalless at half-time, but after the break United seized the initiative as Wayne Rooney headed in Patrice Evra's cross. It was a blow for Arsenal, but Cesc knew there was still time to make amends.

Wenger had reminded his players to make full use of their youthful energy and they came roaring back into the game. Fábregas became more involved in the build-up play and United began to tire. Then, with seven minutes to go, Cesc made his most important contribution, winning possession and finding Rosicky whose cross was buried by van Persie at the back post ahead of Gary Neville. The crowd were jubilant. The young Gunners had rescued yet more points at home with their ability to fight until the final whistle.

Everyone breathed a sigh of relief, but Fábregas set his sights on three points. United had been deflated by van Persie's equaliser and were there for the taking. Tiredness was forgotten as adrenalin took over and Cesc searched for the knockout blow. It came in injury time. Eboue broke free on the right and his cross was inch perfect for Henry to head past van der Sar. It completed a staggering turnaround and presented the Emirates with its most thrilling moment so far. Every Arsenal fan inside the stadium was on their feet to savour the feeling of another famous victory over their deadly rivals. How many times had the Gunners scored in the final fifteen minutes this season? It was beyond belief.

Ferguson was fuming; Wenger beamed with pride. The Frenchman had nothing but praise for his young team after the game: 'I knew after the break we would have a go. They got their goal with their only chance of the half, but we fought back because we have lions in our team. I think we mixed our play well and there was so much spirit in the squad.' Cesc, one of those lions, had not stopped running all afternoon and now he had his reward.

He was understandably ecstatic. It had been an excellent few weeks for the team and suddenly the early season gloom had been lifted. Even the club's youngsters and fringe players had picked up on the positive vibe, as they showed in a rousing Carling Cup semi-final first-leg comeback against Tottenham. Cesc was given a rare run-out in the competition, but things did not start well as Spurs took a 2-0 lead. Nonetheless, Fábregas did not panic and passed as patiently as ever, rebuilding the side's confidence, setting up numerous chances and nursing some of the less experienced players through a rocky first half.

In the second period, the Gunners got their reward as Baptista scored twice to earn Arsenal a draw and make them favourites to close out the tie in the return match.

Fábregas almost won the game late on with a couple of chances, but it was his pass in the build-up to the equaliser that stood out. On a night where a lot of young players were given the chance to shine, nineteen-year-old Cesc had looked like a veteran in midfield and the team were hugely grateful for his calm head under pressure. Such was his vision and movement, nobody had been able to get near the Spaniard in the second half.

Fábregas was clearly delighted with the team's character, telling the media after the match: 'You could see on Sunday against Manchester United we scored two goals in the last ten minutes. Why not in the second half last night? I think all the teams drop a little bit in the last twenty minutes and it is then that we have to push quickly and be stronger offensively. We are showing everyone that even with the young players you can go far in this competition. You have to congratulate them for what they are doing because it is amazing.' It was funny to hear the Spaniard refer to the 'young players' as if he was not one of them.

Cesc refused to get carried away with his good recent form. He spoke to the *Daily Telegraph* in a typically modest fashion: 'I am just nineteen. The good thing about being young is that you've got so many things to learn. Even Thierry [Henry] and Ronaldinho – they can still learn. I need to improve my left foot a lot, improve the defensive side, my heading as well. That has come on lately but, physically, I'm not the biggest man in the world.' He also referred to his failings in front of goal – he was way off track in his bid to score at least ten goals: 'If I had taken thirty per cent of my chances I would have ten goals easy by now.' Instead, not through want of trying, he had just two and both of those had come in August.

The recent win at Blackburn helped dismiss suggestions that the Gunners were weak on their travels against physical teams. Fábregas explained that a team meeting had played a part in sorting out their inconsistency away from home: 'We realised that if we didn't change our mentality we would always struggle in those kinds of games. From then on, we've been showing great character, great attitude and doing really well. We had a talk between ourselves and decided that we had to become more competitive. We all know we can play good football, but this is England and sometimes you have to do other things. I think we're doing that now.'

But Arsenal's inability to kill teams off at home haunted them yet again on 28 January in the FA Cup fourth round against Bolton at the Emirates. Trailing to a Kevin Nolan goal, the Gunners were again indebted to Fábregas for hauling them back into the contest. Cesc forced Jussi Jaaskelainen into one excellent save before making his vital contribution for the team's equaliser. A trademark burst forward resulted in a free-kick just outside the penalty area and Fábregas got up to take it himself. His delivery found its way to Kolo Toure and the Ivorian did the rest. The match ended 1-1. The tie would be decided by a replay at the Reebok Stadium – not one of Arsenal's favourite grounds.

After his exertions over the previous fortnight, Cesc got a well-earned rest against Tottenham in the Carling Cup semi-final second leg as Wenger left the Spaniard on the bench. It was a scrappy contest and the reason Arsenal were not passing the ball as well as they had done in the first leg was easy to spot. Fábregas waited patiently, wondering whether he would be sent into the action. Arsène introduced the midfielder in the seventy-ninth minute, by which time Adebayor had given the Gunners the advantage. Shortly after Cesc's arrival, however, Tottenham equalised through Mido to force extra-time.

Wenger must have cursed. He had not wanted Fábregas to clock up a further half hour that night. Fortunately, a strike from young forward Jeremie Aliadiere and a Pascal Chimbonda own goal settled the semi-final in Arsenal's favour. Cesc joined in the celebrations – he had another trip to the Millennium Stadium to look forward to.

Back in the Premiership, Fábregas and his team-mates found themselves fighting back from a goal down for the umpteenth time at Middlesbrough on 3 February. Senderos was sent off, but Henry's late strike rescued a 1-1 draw. It was an all too familiar story.

Wenger was pleased to see that Cesc did not have far to go to link up with his Spanish colleagues during the international break. Spain were playing England at Old Trafford and so, for once, Fábregas would not be clocking up many air miles. The match, on 7 February, might only have been a friendly, but both teams were keen to record a victory. Cesc would have loved to have started the game, but had to make do with a place on the substitutes' bench. He came on for the final fifteen minutes, by which time Iniesta had put Spain 1-0 up with a fantastic strike, and helped his team-mates hold on for a spirited win. Sadly, Fábregas had no bragging rights when he got back to London: there were no Gunners representatives in the England side. Nonetheless, he was pleased with the way that Spain had performed.

Back in Arsenal uniform, it was a depressingly familiar story for Fábregas. The pressure the Gunners were putting themselves under was no longer a joking matter. Cesc was forever chasing the game because opposing sides were going ahead against Arsenal on a regular basis. It happened again at home to Wigan, who went 1-0 up in the thirty-fifth minute and held on until the closing stages before crumbling to a 2-1 defeat. The visitors were also denied a clear penalty and Wigan boss Paul Jewell was livid to lose out on valuable points in his club's fight for survival. Fábregas was pleased the Gunners had pulled off another comeback, but urged his colleagues to stop leaving it so late.

The FA Cup replay with Bolton on 14 February was next on the agenda for the weary Gunners and Wenger opted to leave Fábregas out of the squad to give the youngster a proper rest. Cesc, Henry and Lehmann remained in London as Arsène put his faith in some of his fringe players. Fábregas desperately wanted to progress in the FA Cup – but all he could do was watch from home. It was another rollercoaster night as the Gunners led from the thirteenth minute, missed a penalty (Gilberto) and then conceded a last-gasp equaliser, which took the game into extra-time. Cesc, though, could breathe easy: Ljungberg and Adebayor both scored, making up for Baptista's missed penalty, the team's second spot-kick of the night, to take the Gunners through to the next round.

Arsenal squared off with Blackburn at the Emirates in the fifth round just three days after their clash with

Bolton, but it turned out to be a frustrating afternoon for Cesc, and one that would boil over at the final whistle. Blackburn had arrived with a game plan to defend in numbers and play physically against the Gunners. Brad Friedel was excellent in the Rovers goal and the visitors received a couple of generous decisions from the referee. Nonetheless, Fábregas should have acknowledged that Blackburn had fought hard and had earned a replay. Instead, he sulked and his temper got the better of him as he lashed out at Rovers boss Mark Hughes – never a good idea.

Cesc had worked his socks off in midfield, despite the close attentions of the Blackburn players, but felt aggrieved that Arsenal had not progressed to the quarter-finals. As he left the field, he made his feelings known to the Blackburn manager, questioning the negativity of the visitors' display. Fábregas wanted to know how, as a former Barcelona player, Hughes could tolerate such a defensive style of play. The Spaniard did not help his cause by wagging his finger in Hughes' direction – it all looked like rather poor sportsmanship. Cesc had been brought up to play attractive football – both in the *cantera* and under Wenger's management – and it frustrated him to see other teams adopting more negative approaches. Yet this was clearly their right. Surely Fábregas did not expect the likes of Blackburn to be expansive against a side containing the likes of himself and Henry? Had the youngster forgotten that Rovers had lost 6-2 at the Emirates earlier in the season: a game in which they had tried to play more positively?

Fortunately, Hughes was in no mood to take the incident further, though he told the press: 'Maybe he

[Fábregas] was frustrated with the way the game went and how he played as an individual, and that he wasn't able to exert as much influence as he normally does. Maybe now he has calmed down, he has understood what we tried to do.' Cesc later apologised to the Rovers boss and Hughes seemed satisfied when he added: 'He's got a winning mentality and we appreciate that. But let's move on.'

It was only at times like these that people remembered that Fábregas was just nineteen years old. He seemed to have been around for ages, but he was still a young man, and while the spat with Hughes may have been childish, it emphasised just how badly he wanted to win and just how highly he regarded playing attractive football. It was the same drive and determination that had led the Spaniard to leave Barcelona for Arsenal in the first place back in 2003. His reaction against Blackburn was fuelled by frustration with himself as much as with anything else.

However, more critical matters lay ahead of Fábregas in the coming weeks. First, the Gunners prepared for the next round of the Champions League. The second round draw had paired Arsenal with PSV Eindhoven of Holland – a tricky tie, but Wenger's side were clear favourites. Cesc was optimistic that his side would prevail, especially with Gallas now back in the starting XI and strengthening the back four since the Blackburn match. Fans were still waiting to see the Gallas-Toure partnership in full flow.

The first leg was in Eindhoven on 20 February and the Gunners travelled with plenty of belief. Unfortunately, they left that belief in the dressing room on what was a damaging European night. PSV won the match 1-0 and stopped Arsenal from finding their rhythm, though Fábregas went close with a shot from the edge of the penalty area. Neither side created many chances, but it was the Dutchmen who brought a slender advantage to the Emirates for the second leg: if they scored an away goal, the Gunners would be in big trouble.

Fábregas put the disappointment to one side as Arsenal faced Chelsea at the weekend in the Carling Cup final. True to his word, Wenger kept faith with his fringe players and youngsters, mixing in a few first-team stars. Cesc made the starting line-up alongside fellow young guns Theo Walcott, Armand Traoré and Denilson, against a Chelsea side packed with internationals. It was a massive day for the club. Though the Carling Cup had been undervalued by a number of teams, Cesc wanted to win every prize available and his hunger for silverware saw him fired up for the final.

Walcott handed Arsenal the perfect start but, though Cesc urged the team to stay focused, Drogba soon equalised for the Blues. The drama continued in the second half when Terry was rushed to hospital after swallowing his tongue. It was a stomach-churning moment and left a number of players feeling queasy. Chelsea recovered quickest and Drogba pounced to score the winner with six minutes to go, breaking Arsenal hearts.

Emotions boiled over late on as the Gunners tried in vain to level the scores. A fourteen-man brawl led to red cards for Arsenal's Toure and Adebayor and John Obi Mikel of Chelsea. Fábregas needlessly got himself involved with Lampard, earning himself a yellow card, and the Spaniard also confronted Drogba and Mourinho as referee Howard Webb struggled to keep control of the players. The unseemly finale to the match spoiled what had otherwise been an intriguing battle. Cesc's temper had again got the better of him and it was something he needed to address. The Gunners collected their runners-up medals in dejected fashion and prepared to travel back to London empty-handed.

Looking back at the Carling Cup final, former Gunner Paul Merson was very critical of Fábregas' behaviour in Cardiff. Merson wrote in the *Evening Standard*: 'Cesc Fábregas has to learn to calm down if he is ever going to become an Arsenal great. It was very disappointing to see his petulant behaviour against Chelsea and it is becoming a worrying trend. The nineteen-year-old Spaniard has bags of ability, but it is being undermined by his own temper and his inability to control it. Everyone gets wound up during matches and the midfielder has made a habit of being in the headlines for all the wrong reasons in recent weeks.'

Merson, who was also referring to Cesc's bust-up with Blackburn boss Hughes, felt that Fábregas' outbursts were unnecessary and reflected badly on him. Yes, the Spaniard hated to lose, but he had to control his emotions, otherwise he would quickly earn a bad reputation, and one that would be difficult to shed. Wenger was aware of the situation, but let the youngster work out his issues independently before he thought about getting involved.

A miserable week for the Gunners was completed with a 1-0 defeat away to Blackburn in their FA Cup fifth-round replay. Rovers came out as if fuelled by Fábregas' outburst ten days earlier and a late Benni McCarthy goal ended Arsenal's hopes of a domestic cup triumph and put additional pressure on Wenger's players ahead of the Champions League second-round second-leg match against PSV the following week. Perhaps with one eye on that fixture, Arsène had chosen to rest several players, including Fábregas and Henry, for the trip to Ewood Park and the Gunners had paid for that decision. Without Cesc, the midfield was flat and provided little service for the front men. Wenger was clearly throwing all his resources into the club's Champions League bid.

A 2-1 win at home to Reading came as a welcome boost for the players, even if it was not a particularly memorable day for Fábregas. For once, the Emirates crowd witnessed the home side take the lead as a Gilberto penalty set Arsenal on their way, before Baptista doubled the advantage. Cesc was back in the starting line-up and the improvement from the midweek loss was obvious. With the game seemingly sealed, Fábregas contrived to end his goal-scoring drought by putting the ball into his own net from a corner. He was a relieved man when the final whistle went and the three points were secured. Having earlier fluffed a simple chance in front of goal, it was an afternoon to forget for the Spaniard.

On 7 March, all eyes were fixed on the Emirates again as PSV arrived for the second leg of their European tie, leading 1-0 from the first game. After their Carling Cup final defeat and their FA Cup elimination – not to mention their Premiership woes – the Gunners were well aware that the Champions League represented their only remaining chance of silverware. The clash with PSV had suddenly taken on even greater significance.

Even though Cesc and company were regarded as a stronger outfit, there was plenty of anxiety around the Emirates. A crowd of 60,073 poured through the gates, hoping for an emphatic Arsenal display, but fearing that it could be a nail-biting night. Fábregas remained confident, as usual, and Wenger showed faith in his young charges by picking Denilson to partner Cesc in midfield.

After a tight first half, Arsenal got the all-important breakthrough just before the hour mark when Brazilian defender Alex diverted the ball into his own net from a corner. The Gunners were level in the tie. Fábregas quickly looked to take the game by the scruff of the neck, feeding Adebayor, whose effort was well saved, and then getting into a good position himself, only to blaze over. Henry had been summoned from the bench as Wenger tried in vain to avoid a tense finish.

As everyone began to think about the possibility of extra-time, the unthinkable happened. PSV won a free-kick on the left and Alex made amends for his earlier own goal by heading the cross past Lehmann. That made it 1-1 on the night, 2-1 on aggregate. There were seven minutes to go and the Gunners now needed to score twice to stay in the competition. Fábregas tried his best, but deep down he knew that there was no coming back from Alex's goal. Arsenal would not be repeating their 2006 Champions League final appearance; the Gunners' season was lying in tatters.

A distraught Wenger told the media: 'It's cruel. We lacked a bit of sharpness and, of course, we lacked a bit of quality in the final third. We can only think we played the game we wanted to play, but we didn't take our chances.'

The fact that Alex, the match-winner, was a player owned by Chelsea and on loan to PSV rubbed salt into the Gunners' wounds. The dressing room was a quiet and miserable place after the game as the implications of elimination sunk in for Cesc and his colleagues.

Just three weeks earlier, everything had looked rosy for Arsenal; now Wenger had to lift his players for a strong finish to the Premiership season. With no silverware to focus on, it was a strange feeling for Fábregas. Nonetheless, the Gunners were good enough to beat Aston Villa 1-0 at Villa Park with Abu Diaby grabbing a fortuitous winner. Cesc was excellent in midfield, enjoying the space he was afforded by his Villa counterparts and stroking the ball around with ease. With Henry seemingly out injured for the rest of the season, Fábregas wanted to show that he could take on the extra responsibility.

In midweek, the Gunners found themselves on the wrong end of a 1-0 scoreline as Andy Johnson's late winner earned Everton the three points at Goodison Park. Cesc was a constant menace through the game, but some of his team-mates had off days on Merseyside. Arsenal stayed third as Liverpool could only manage a draw in an earlier kick-off, but that did little to improve the mood on the journey home. Fábregas had lost count of the number of silly goals and missed chances he and his team-mates had suffered over the course of the season, and he knew that they had cost the side dearly.

International commitments gave Cesc a welcome bolthole from the chaos at Arsenal. It allowed him to unwind a little with the rest of the Spanish camp and forget about the Gunners' plight. Spain faced Denmark and Iceland in crucial Euro 2008 qualifiers and, after the morale-denting losses to Northern Ireland and Sweden, Fábregas needed no reminding how important these fixtures were. As he joined up with his compatriots, he revealed how comfortable he now felt in the Spanish squad: 'Since the coach took me [into the squad] it has been fifteen games. He has picked me in every game since then and I have played in every one of them, even if it's just one minute, ten minutes or from the start. That is really important for me, because it shows he has a lot of confidence in me.'

However, Cesc remained an unused substitute for the clash with Denmark on 24 March. Spain outlasted the Danes to win 2-1 with goals from Fernando Morientes and David Villa. Had Cesc fallen down the pecking order in the manager's eyes? Iniesta had taken Fábregas' midfield role for this match, but perhaps Aragones was just rotating his squad.

Nevertheless, Cesc was pleased with the solid victory which set the players up well for the clash with Iceland just four days later. After the stuttering start to their Euro 2008 campaign, Fábregas realised it was imperative to bounce back immediately, otherwise the Spaniards would fall behind the leaders in Group F. The win over Denmark had been a step in the right direction, but picking up another three points against Iceland was imperative.

Spain did indeed make it two wins in four days, but needed a late winner from Iniesta to clinch the victory. It was far from the team's best display, making it all the more surprising that Fábregas was left on the bench for the full ninety minutes for the second successive match.

On the positive side, the earlier defeats to Northern Ireland and Sweden had been forgotten and everyone in the Spanish camp was focused on the rest of the qualifying campaign.

The backlash from the Spanish public and media would have been unbearable if the squad failed to qualify for Euro 2008. Fábregas knew this only too well and vowed not to let the team suffer that fate. There were plenty of games left and he remained confident that Spain would still top the group. This, added to the obvious incentive of playing at Euro 2008, spurred on Cesc and the rest of the Spain squad and the midfielder was desperate to win back his place in the starting line-up for the next fixture.

Erratic results also marred the next week as it became clear that now there were no trophies on offer, the Gunners were suffering from a lack of motivation. A 4-1 defeat at Liverpool on 31 March was a perfect indication of just how far the team had slipped. Peter Crouch scored a hat-trick and took advantage of an Arsenal performance which lacked both belief and spirit. Fábregas helped create the team's consolation goal – his corner eventually fell to Gallas who bundled the ball home – but otherwise it was another grim day for the London side and, to make matters worse, Liverpool moved above them into third place.

Things did not improve the following weekend either as Arsenal suffered their first Premiership defeat at the Emirates against relegation-threatened West Ham. Fábregas' luck was well and truly out this season in terms of goalscoring. He had struck the woodwork or been denied by brilliant saves so often during the campaign and against the Hammers he beat the superb Robert Green with a fine drive, only to see the ball crash back off the crossbar. He also forced Green into a good save from a header. What more could he do? The team was struggling to score goals without Thierry Henry, which was a major concern considering the constant reports linking the Frenchman with a move abroad. A 0-0 draw in midweek with Newcastle only served to emphasise the crisis Henry's exit might cause.

Finally, on 14 April, Arsenal got back to winning ways. After one victory from their last six games prior to their clash with Bolton, Fábregas knew the Gunners desperately needed the three points to raise morale – and so he chose this match to re-discover his scoring boots. Initially, it was a typical Arsenal home game. The visitors had taken the lead and the Gunners were desperately fighting back. Rosicky equalised and then, just after half-time, Fábregas stepped into the limelight to score his first Premiership goal of the season – and his first in any competition since August. He burst onto a through ball and calmly put the Gunners ahead. It was incredible to think that it had taken him this long to open his account. He and his team-mates hung onto the advantage and the Emirates was a much cheerier place.

As they always say, as with London buses, you wait ages for one and then several come along at once. No sooner had Cesc netted his first league goal of the season than he was on the scoresheet again. In the next home game, against Manchester City, he scored Arsenal's crucial second goal to set up a 3-1 victory. The ball fell to Fábregas 25 yards out and, with his confidence sky high, he fired a shot into the net. It had been a memorable week for him. Cesc may have left it until late in the season, but he was now producing complete midfield displays. He had always wanted to contribute a double-figure goal tally, but things had not been falling his way.

Wenger acknowledged that Fábregas' strike had been crucial: 'I think we deserved the victory as we created a lot of chances and when we got our second it made it easier because they had to change their shape.' The Arsenal boss hoped that his midfielder could improve his tally next season.

A trip to White Hart Lane should have brought a third consecutive win for the Gunners, but a late goal from Jermaine Jenas earned the home side a 2-2 draw. Fábregas' deliveries from set-pieces had been immaculate all afternoon and he was the provider for both Arsenal goals.

Determined to finish the season strongly for their supporters, the team pressed on. The 3-1 scoreline at home to Fulham on 29 April did not tell the full story as the Gunners needed two late goals to clinch the three points. Fábregas collected one assist and might have had more if the strikers had been more prolific. Although Arsenal had won their last three games at the Emirates, Cesc knew the team's home record would have to improve next season if they wanted to challenge United and Chelsea for the title. They had simply drawn too often at their new stadium.

The Gunners had one final opportunity to bask in the spotlight as Chelsea arrived on the penultimate weekend of the season, needing a victory to keep their title hopes alive. Anything less would send the Premiership trophy back to Manchester. Wenger had had his problems with both Ferguson and Mourinho in recent years, so could not be accused of any favouritism.

Fábregas recalled the pain of losing the Carling Cup final to the Blues and wanted to make amends. He knew he had gone too far with his involvement in the scuffle in the closing seconds of that game and was determined to show how much he had matured. A win would be a fitting way for the Gunners to complete their home fixtures for the campaign. When Khalid Boulahrouz was sent off after fouling Baptista in the box just before half-time and Gilberto converted the spot-kick, it looked all over for Chelsea. The champions had a mountain to climb. Though no one in the Arsenal squad was excited at the thought of United lifting the trophy, there seemed a great desire to win the match and stop Mourinho's side from retaining the title. The celebrations when Gilberto opened the scoring told the full story. This was far from a meaningless end-of-season contest.

Chelsea responded heroically in the second half and, led by Michael Essien, threatened to defy the odds. The Ghanaian powered forward to head an equaliser, giving the Blues twenty minutes to keep their title dreams alive. Fábregas was typically busy at the heart of the Arsenal midfield and twice created chances that could have settled the match in the Gunners' favour. In the end, although Cesc had to settle for a 1-1 draw, he and his team-mates could take solace in the knowledge that they had been the ones who denied Jose Mourinho a third successive title. Sir Alex Ferguson could uncork the champagne – United were champions again after a three-year wait.

The final match of the season was a 0-0 draw at

Fratton Park against Portsmouth. After the emotions of the clash with Chelsea, the Gunners were not on top form, but there was still plenty of drama. Wenger fielded a young line-up, taking the chance to test some of his fledglings, but Cesc was not one of the first-team players to sit out. He took his place in midfield and was influential in crafting the string of chances that Arsenal missed in the first half. Baptista missed a penalty as well as a good chance from a Fábregas free-kick.

Portsmouth were still scrapping for a UEFA Cup spot, but as Arsenal stood firm, the home side saw their hopes slip away. From Cesc's point of view, this match summed up the team's season – too many missed chances. He was sick of reading and hearing about it. Enough was enough. The team had dropped so many points due to poor finishing and Fábregas knew he was one of the culprits.

The draw with Portsmouth meant that the Gunners finished fourth in the Premiership table, a humiliating twenty-one points behind Manchester United. Arsenal had started the season poorly and had never threatened to join the title race, leaving United and Chelsea to fight for the trophy. Liverpool ended on the same points total as Arsenal, but sat third on goal difference.

Several things stood out when Cesc looked at the final standings. Firstly, the Gunners had drawn eleven league games during the course of the season – too many for a title-chasing side – and a number of those draws had come at the Emirates. Eight defeats was also a bad statistic. Secondly, Wenger's Arsenal teams have always had a reputation for being free-scoring, yet they had found the net fewer times than Mourinho's functional

Chelsea side. United had struck twenty more goals than the Gunners. It was further evidence of all the wasted chances that had marred the campaign for Fábregas and the rest of the squad. Once again they would have to get through a qualifying tie to secure their place in next season's Champions League.

On a positive note, in terms of his individual performances, it had been a good year for Cesc. He had been the brightest light in the Arsenal side on numerous occasions and his passing and understanding with his team-mates was getting better and better. He had been superb in securing two victories over United during the campaign – and two draws against Chelsea. It showed just how much he loved the big occasion and how he refused to be intimidated by the prospect of facing other top-class players.

His displays were recognised with a second-place finish in the voting for PFA Young Player of the Year. Cristiano Ronaldo won this award – along with the PFA Player of the Year accolade – after his superb performances for United. Having played over fifty times during the campaign, Cesc had won plenty of admirers across the country and he was delighted to have been in contention for such a prestigious honour.

Fábregas resolved to enjoy his summer break and come back for the new season raring to go. Considering his involvement with the Spanish World Cup squad, it had been a long two years for the young Spaniard. He had had little time to relax, but was determined to help the Gunners make a stronger start to the next campaign and push United and Chelsea all the way for the Premiership crown. If they were to do so, much would depend on

Cesc. The youngster was now widely regarded as the team's most important player.

The Spaniard had mentioned several times during the course of the season that it would be important for him to have a rest over the summer months to ensure that he did not burn out. On one occasion he told the media: 'I am looking forward to this summer. Sometimes I do think I need one summer just to rest. I remember when I was sixteen turning seventeen, I had seven weeks rest and I came back in pre-season refreshed and ready to go. That is what made the difference because I was a reserve player and I came into the first team in this period, and because I had rested I had a lot of energy and power.' The trouble was, he now had international duty to think of and that often ruined any summer holiday plans he might have had.

Shortly after the end of the Premiership season, Fábregas was once more in action with the Spanish national team. He did not feature in the 2-0 win away to Latvia on 2 June – the third consecutive qualifier he had been left on the bench – but returned to the starting line-up in Liechtenstein on 6 June. He was replaced after sixty-eight minutes, but not before he had conjured Spain's opening goal for Villa. The 2-0 victory over Liechtenstein made it four qualifying wins in a row and the team's prospects looked very bright.

But any hopes Fábregas may have had of spending a few peaceful weeks following international duty were dashed when reports began to circulate linking him with a move to Real Madrid. Cesc had wanted to switch off from football and these rumours were far from welcome. The media in England and Spain latched onto the story and it was all over the newspapers.

When Fábregas did eventually speak on the matter, he made it clear that he had no plans to leave Arsenal – mainly because he wanted to keep working with Arsène Wenger. Cesc told the press: 'I am only twenty and all I have to do is enjoy my football and improve – and I want to do that with this team. I will try to win titles with Arsenal and give my all to Arsène Wenger. I will always be grateful to him for giving me my chance.' This was the kind of committed response Gunners supporters had wanted to hear from Patrick Vieira when he was swayed by interest from abroad in the summer of 2005.

He has since referred back to this interest from Real Madrid. Discussing the topic in November 2007, Fábregas promised that the huge wages offered by the likes of Real would not persuade him to leave Arsenal: 'It's nothing to do with money. If it was I would have gone to Real Madrid last summer. Nor did I go to Arsenal and say: "I've got an offer, give me more money." I am not moved by money, I am moved by football. People said I left Barcelona to go to Arsenal for the money and now they are having to eat their words. I came to become a good footballer, to grow, to play at the highest level.'

He had done just that and he was about to enjoy his best season to date.

CHAPTER 6
TEAM TALISMAN

During the summer of 2007, the inevitable happened: Thierry Henry completed his on-off move to Barcelona for £16.2 million. Wenger paid Thierry a fitting tribute and then concentrated on the new era. The departure of Henry opened the way for Fábregas to take control of the team's passing style. It was a role and responsibility he relished. Just as he had stepped up after Vieira's exit in 2005, Cesc seized the chance to become the side's talisman with both hands.

While William Gallas would be officially named the new Gunners skipper prior to the start of the campaign, it was Fábregas who would be charged with ensuring that Wenger's flowing, attacking approach was preserved. After all, it was Arsène's trademark and the Frenchman had no hesitation in throwing more responsibility in Cesc's direction. The torch was being passed from the departed Henry to Fábregas. The young Spaniard was now the symbol of Arsenal's future.

As Andy Dunn of the *People* put it: 'A Spanish giant came pounding on the Emirates front door in the summer, wanting to drag away Arsenal's most sublime talent. And we all know what happened ... he stayed.' Dunn was not referring to Henry's switch to Barcelona, but to Fábregas' decision to reject Real Madrid. The reporter added: 'Henry is the history of Wenger's reign, Fábregas is the future.'

It was an exciting new era at the Emirates and the Spaniard would be leading from the front. It was a young squad that lined up for the team's pre-season photo and the media were not predicting big things from Wenger's fledglings. Arsène thought otherwise, though. He explained to reporters that his players 'can achieve what they want and desire'. To clarify the meaning of this comment, he added: 'That means win the Premiership and win all kinds of trophies they want to win. The hunger in the team is strong, my hunger is stronger than ever and the talent and the potential of the team are very high.'

The Frenchman also revealed that there would be a change of approach at the club in the wake of Henry's exit. In an interview with *Four Four Two*, Wenger said: 'When you have a player of his [Henry's] importance with such a young team, the play was always going to go through him. When he wanted the ball, he got the ball. Now he's not there anymore, everybody has to take the initiative and express themselves a little bit more.'

Fábregas agreed with Wenger, telling the *Guardian*: 'Thierry is the best I've ever played with. There's no doubt. But there was this other factor. When I came I felt I was low and he was high and for a long time I was intimidated. When I had the ball I felt I had no choice but to look for him. He has such a strong character that he almost made you feel this way. I needed him to say, "Look, you don't always have to play the ball to me." Once he said that, I was free and I gave him even more assists.' Cesc wished the striker well at Barcelona and would, of course, be tracking the team's progress keenly. He had spoken to Henry about the positives and negatives of the move and had told him about what to expect at the Catalan club.

Meanwhile, back in England, the Gunners were being written off by sections of the press. But Cesc was happy with the 'outsiders' tag and hoped to surprise people. A number of the Arsenal players had taken a little time to adapt to Premiership football, but Fábregas saw that they were now ready to take the league by storm – even if the average age of the team was very young.

While Kolo Toure and Gallas formed a solid, experienced central defensive partnership, elsewhere the Arsenal team looked green. Adebayor and van Persie would be expected to fill Henry's boots, while Fábregas, Flamini, Hleb and Rosicky would support the more-seasoned legs of Gilberto Silva in midfield. Challenging in four competitions appeared a big ask considering the inexperience in the team.

Yet Cesc has never backed down from a challenge. If anything he revelled in his senior role, knowing that he would be called upon more frequently to provide key contributions. Within the space of a few years, he had gone from promising youngster to vital match-winner. Wenger worried that he was placing too much pressure on his young Spaniard, but felt Fábregas could handle it.

Since his arrival from Barcelona back in 2003, Cesc had done little to disappoint the Arsenal boss and the Spaniard was keen to keep it that way.

The major component missing from Fábregas' midfield displays in the past few years had been a lack of goals and now he had been given a greater licence to shoot. He vowed to improve this area of his game and better the measly four goals he had scored during the 2006/07 campaign. Two of those goals had come in a Champions League qualifier in August and the other two were in April; the long drought in between needed to be addressed. After all, there was absolutely no reason why he could not achieve a tally of 15 goals for the season. Cristiano Ronaldo had enjoyed a breakout scoring run last season – now Cesc had to put together a similar streak to put the Gunners into the title picture.

Arsène attempted to address the situation during the close season. As Fábregas revealed in his interview with Jonathan Northcroft of *The Sunday Times*, Wenger gave him some guidance prior to the start of the campaign: 'The boss told me, "You have to be calm." He showed me a video tape and said, "See? You have more time than you think." Before there was something in my head saying "Score!" and I wanted to do things too quick, without thinking.'

The summer transfer market was not overly busy for the Gunners. Wenger did not make big-name signings to replace Henry, instead preferring to spread the money around on Croatian international Eduardo Da Silva, who had scored for his country against England, and French full-back Bacary Sagna. Both players were relatively unknown to Premiership fans across England.

Would they really improve the squad? Not everyone was convinced.

Elsewhere, their fellow title challengers were looking strong. Manchester United had been the biggest spenders, adding youngsters Nani and Anderson and England international Owen Hargreaves. Ferguson also completed a loan move for Argentine Carlos Tevez, who had been at the centre of controversy during his stint at West Ham. At Anfield, Liverpool were welcoming several new faces, including Spanish striker Fernando Torres. Cesc knew all about Torres' quality from his involvement in the international squad and felt the former Atletico Madrid forward would be a huge success on Merseyside. Chelsea, meanwhile, had their quietest summer since the arrival of Abramovich, with Florent Malouda, costing around £13.5 million, the only big-money addition to the squad. But everyone expected more from Michael Ballack and Andriy Shevchenko, who had flattered to deceive the previous year.

The mood around the Emirates was not helped by some negative comments from within the Arsenal dressing room. Among the dissenters was Gallas, who questioned the club's ambition in the wake of Henry's departure: 'What is sure is that several players are questioning the club's future. Around us, all the teams are recruiting, but what is planned to compensate for the departure of Henry? It is necessary to recruit players of reputation because young players have many qualities but the season is very long.' Gallas' outburst was strangely rewarded in due course with the captain's armband.

Such issues were of little concern to Cesc, though he

much preferred to see the dressing room united. He simply got his head down and worked hard to ensure he was at peak fitness for the long campaign ahead. Wenger had made it clear to Fábregas that he would get few rests over the coming ten months. In past campaigns, Arsène had tried to give the Spaniard a breather every now and again as the youngster developed and adapted to the English game. Now, though, the Frenchman knew he would rarely be able to leave Cesc out of the line-up.

The season began at home to Fulham on 12 August as the Gunners prepared for life after Thierry and their second season at their new ground. Fábregas was itching for the 2007/08 campaign to kick off. The team made a far from convincing start, though, as the visitors grabbed a very early lead. Cesc and his team-mates had to dig deep to fight back and they completed a dramatic turnaround with just minutes remaining. Van Persie – from the penalty spot – and Hleb scored the goals, but Fábregas' endeavours in midfield were pivotal in the comeback. A nail-biting afternoon had been rescued and Wenger spoke proudly of his 'resilient' players after the final whistle. Lehmann was the most relieved man in the ground as it was his error that had allowed Fulham to go ahead.

The Gunners made a strong start to their Champions League campaign, winning 2-0 in the first leg of their qualifier against Sparta Prague, a game that saw Cesc open his goal-scoring account for the season, netting Arsenal's first goal and making life easier for the return leg at the Emirates. The feeling of finding the net would become addictive for him in the months ahead.

Fábregas and his colleagues were back in Premiership

action on 19 August. A 1-1 draw at Blackburn was a frustrating result as the Gunners had dominated large chunks of the contest. Lehmann was again the villain of the piece as he gifted Rovers their equaliser. Ultimately, the German stopper would pay the price for his blunders as Manuel Almunia was given another chance to impress. An injury to Gallas added to Wenger's unhappiness. Cesc had played a part in Arsenal's opener and felt disappointed to be leaving Lancashire with only a point.

A trip to Athens in midweek meant it was a hectic time for Fábregas. The Greeks beat Spain 3-2 on the night and Cesc could do little to salvage the match as he was only brought on in the eighty-second minute with the team trailing 3-1. David Albelda, of Valencia, and Xavi took the starting midfield berths, leaving Cesc to watch from the sidelines. He hoped that if he kept performing well in the Premiership, he could win back a starting role.

Some speculated as to whether playing his club football outside Spain was hindering his chances at international level and whether Aragones had a preference for those who he could easily keep tabs on in La Liga. It was an interesting issue and simply underlined one of the dangers involved in moving to a foreign league. The likes of Albelda, Xavi and Iniesta were in the public eye more often than Xabi Alonso and Fábregas, and it did not seem to be working in the English-based players' favour.

Back in action for Arsenal at home to Manchester City, Fábregas continued his fine form. The managerial appointment of Swede Sven Goran Eriksson had given City a new look, and they arrived at the Emirates full of confidence. In what turned out to be a tight contest, it needed a special moment to decide the outcome. Arsenal fans groaned in disbelief when van Persie's penalty was saved by Kasper Schmeichel – son of Peter – with twenty-five minutes to go. Was it going to be one of those days? Fortunately, for Wenger, Fábregas refused to accept a 0-0 scoreline and on one of his increasingly regular bursts from midfield, the Spaniard decided the match in the eightieth minute. His crisp finish gave evidence of his desire to score more goals. It was the first goal City had conceded in the 2007/08 campaign and underlined the improvements in his shooting technique.

There was noticeable character in the Arsenal performance as they searched for the knockout blow and results such as this augured well for their title challenge. Cesc was delighted to have earned his team three points, as was Wenger, who praised his players: 'I know we'll fight until the last second. We look solid and strong and mentally very focused and they are good signs.' The clean sheet was also significant as the Gunners were keen to tighten up their defensive efforts.

Arsène even found time to discuss Fábregas' individual performance and praised the Spaniard's all-round contribution to the side: 'Cesc will score more goals. But this was a goal that did not come from a chance. And while other midfielders may score more, Cesc contributes more in the way of assists.' The Spaniard was the clear choice as Man of the Match for his role in the narrow win and hoped it would be the first of many times that he headed for the dressing room with a bottle of champagne in his hands.

In an interview with the *Guardian* in late August, Fábregas revealed his emotions over his whirlwind career to date at the club: 'I came to London in September 2003 and so next week it will be four years since I left Barcelona for Arsenal. Everything has come so quickly that it's unbelievable. I was sixteen then and now I am twenty. A lot has changed.'

Cesc added an outline of the aims he had when he joined the club and the sacrifices that were required along the way: 'I am proud of how I coped, but I knew what I wanted even before I came here. I knew if I had to be alone for two years then I could do it – as long as it meant first-team football. If I could show everybody what I could do on the pitch then there would be no problem at all with the loneliness.' Fábregas had certainly established himself and the Gunners were reaping the benefits.

It was onwards and upwards for Cesc. Out on the pitch, another confident defensive display kept Sparta Prague at bay in midweek. A 3-0 scoreline put Arsenal through to the draw for the group stage, much to the relief of everyone associated with the club. A season without Champions League participation would have been disastrous. Wenger opted to keep Fábregas on the bench, hoping that it would be an easy night. With the Gunners in control at 1-0 – and 3-0 on aggregate – Cesc was introduced to the action. It was no surprise to see the Spaniard immediately at the heart of the team's best moves and Fábregas scored Arsenal's second late on. He already had three goals to his name and it was only August. Still, he had begun last season with a few goals and had then failed to build on it. There was nothing to get excited about yet.

The following weekend he took his tally to four. Portsmouth were the visitors and Fábregas struck the second of the Gunners' three goals in a fine 3-1 victory. Senderos was harshly sent off just after half-time for a professional foul, but it made little difference. An unbeaten start to the campaign in all competitions was exactly what Arsène had wanted from his players.

Cesc and his team-mates received good news in early September as Wenger signed a contract extension at the club, keeping him at the Emirates until 2011. There had been some nervy moments for Fábregas when it looked as though Arsène might leave, but now he had committed to developing this young team. The Arsenal boss told the media: 'My heart is tied to this football club, so signing a new deal was always my intention. Arsenal is the club of my life. I have a responsibility to the fans to deliver silverware and also a responsibility to the players to help turn our potential into prizes.' This, along with the side's good start to the season, meant that Fábregas and his colleagues were on a high.

The only frustration for Cesc at this stage of the season was the lack of opportunities he received from Aragones on the international stage. Named in the Spanish squad to face Iceland, Fábregas could only watch from the bench as Spain collected a 1-1 draw from the trip. He had not played a minute in four of the last five qualifiers and was a little baffled by his lack of playing time. Admittedly, there was a lot of competition for midfield berths, but Cesc had been on outstanding form for Arsenal in recent weeks. A few days later, yet another ninety minutes on the sidelines added to the disappointment – this time Spain picked up a win in his absence, beating Latvia 2-0 in Oviedo.

Back in England, Fábregas was at least fresh for

Arsenal action. Trips to White Hart Lane have always been highlights for Cesc and it is the type of fixture he looks for first when the schedule for the season is published. On 15 September, the Gunners travelled the short distance in good form while, contrastingly, Tottenham were struggling, with manager Martin Jol under fire. It would be one of the toughest tests of this new-look Arsenal side. Fábregas would go toe-to-toe with fellow fledglings Jermaine Jenas and Tom Huddlestone – the midfield areas promised to be vital.

And on this day, Cesc would once again prove his worth. With the Gunners trailing to a Gareth Bale strike, Fábregas refused to be flustered and would not be moved from his usual patient, passing approach. Gradually, Arsenal wore Tottenham down and, after Adebayor equalised, Wenger became noticeably more relaxed on the touchline. He would soon come to rely on the fighting spirit evident throughout the side. For several years, the Gunners had struggled on their Premiership travels, but this current crop of players seemed to be made of sterner stuff. They would not lie down for anyone.

Then came a moment that illustrated just how far Fábregas had developed. He was desperate to contribute more goals – there was no secret about that – and he chose the perfect moment to continue his scoring streak. Collecting the ball just inside the Tottenham half, he was not closed down. As no challenge arrived, he surged on towards goal and unleashed a ferocious strike that left Paul Robinson with no chance.

Fábregas raced over to the Arsenal fans to celebrate the moment. His team-mates followed and the passions of a North London derby were evident for all to see. With just ten minutes remaining, Cesc's strike had seemingly decided the outcome of the match. Adebayor struck an impressive third goal late on as the team kept their unbeaten run alive. Wenger was thrilled after the match, telling reporters: 'It shows our spirit and belief. There is something in the side; quality, of course, but also mental strength.'

In an article in the *Daily Mirror*, Martin Lipton reported the special praise Arsène had reserved for Fábregas: 'If it becomes hectic, he keeps his head and cools the game down when it becomes a bit nervous. Suddenly he finds a good pass and gets you out of tight situations.' Lipton himself called Cesc 'the boy-man' and added: 'Fábregas may only be twenty, but in his head he is already thirty-two, chillingly calm amid the maelstrom and utterly outstanding.' It was not only the Spaniard's ability to pass the ball effectively that made him so elusive in the centre of midfield. His movement was equally impressive as he always managed to get himself into space to receive possession – not necessarily acres of space, but enough to take a touch, get his head up and find a team-mate. It was uncanny how often he found himself with no opposition player within five yards of him. With his perfect control, balance and technique, it provided him with more than enough room in which to hurt opponents with his ability.

The Gunners were winning over the doubters, and pundits who had written off their title hopes were being forced to re-think their opinion. Much of this was due to the performances of Fábregas at the heart of the midfield. He had been sensational so far. Cesc had seen nothing in the first few months of the season to persuade him that Arsenal were not good enough to win silverware during the campaign: 'I believe we can win one of the major ones [trophies], like the Premier League or the Champions League. It has been two years since we have won a trophy and that is too long for Arsenal. I cannot even think about a third year like that.'

He added: 'We have to be lucky with injuries and things like that. But we have learned together, we have gained experience together. I know them [his team-mates] all – and we are all winners. Even if it means we stay at home every night and just concentrate on football, then that is what we have to do.' Here was yet more evidence that silverware, rather than money or celebrity status, was Fábregas' motivation. It would be interesting to see whether he could back up these comments with match-winning performances.

The Champions League group stage draw had placed Arsenal in Group H along with Sevilla of Spain, Steaua Bucharest and Slavia Prague. Cesc fancied the team's chances of reaching the knockout rounds. The journey to reach the second round began on 19 September at home to Sevilla who, like the Gunners, were famed for their attacking style of play. Unfortunately for the Spaniards, they met an Arsenal side on top form. Fábregas was once again in the thick of the action. His strike was deflected into the net by Sevilla defender Julien Escude to give the Gunners the lead just before the half-hour mark. Cesc's free-kick then created a chance for van Persie who made it 2-0.

To put the icing on the cake, Fábregas was also involved in the build-up for the third goal, scored by new boy Eduardo. Arsenal had been irresistible on the night and some suggested that the team was stronger as a whole now that Henry had gone. The players were taking the initiative themselves more often, rather than relying on the Frenchman's magic. Cesc had certainly lifted his performances to a new level.

It was great timing on the Spaniard's part. Prior to the Sevilla clash, Wenger had taken time away from his preparations to heap praise on Fábregas and the resemblance that he bore to one of France's greatest ever players, Michel Platini. Arsène told the media: 'His [Cesc's] vision is comparable to Platini. Cesc has it all in front of him, but he has a vision. He will still develop. I remember Platini was more of a striker and Cesc is more of a midfielder. He is adding that element to his game, but Platini had more of a striker's mentality. Cesc is a guy who likes to be at the heart of things.'

It was very flattering for Fábregas to be compared to Platini – a man who had won the European Footballer of the Year award on three occasions during his illustrious career. The French legend's glory years may have come a bit before Cesc's time, but the youngster knew all about the playmaker's reputation in the game. Wenger clearly felt the Spaniard possessed the inner belief to reach the highest level.

The following weekend, Fábregas struck again. It was becoming a trend. Premiership newcomers Derby received little sympathy at the Emirates as the Gunners smashed five goals past them, with Adebayor bagging a hat-trick. Cesc scored Arsenal's fourth and played some sumptuous passes, one of which released Adebayor for the Togo front man's first goal of the afternoon. It was one of the easiest games in recent memory for Wenger's side, but it was impossible to ignore the swagger with which the Gunners were performing. Cesc was thrilled to have found the net once again and vowed to continue his hot streak.

Having sat out Arsenal's Carling Cup victory over Sam Allardyce's Newcastle, Fábregas returned to the fray against West Ham at Upton Park on 29 September, keen to protect the Gunners' unbeaten start to the season. The previous season, the team had suffered a 1-0 defeat away to the Hammers in the match that saw Arsène Wenger and Alan Pardew apparently squaring up to one another on the touchline. This time Arsenal recorded a 1-0 win. Van Persie was the match-winner, heading Hleb's cross past Robert Green in the West Ham goal. With Gallas still out injured, the Gunners had to work hard as a unit defensively and Cesc put in a solid shift in midfield. They were eager to get their captain fit again, but the back four were letting no one down with their play.

A fifth consecutive clean sheet followed away to Steaua Bucharest in Europe in a match where Fábregas should have added to his goals tally but wasted one glorious opportunity. Van Persie struck with fourteen minutes to go to earn Arsenal a 1-0 victory. Van Persie continued his hot streak the following weekend in a 3-2 win against Roy Keane's Sunderland. The Dutchman scored twice, including the decisive strike in the eightieth minute. Cesc had looked in menacing form all afternoon and it was a foul on Fábregas that led to the opening goal. Van Persie lashed home the resulting free-kick. The three points put Arsenal top of the table again and kept belief high in the squad.

October saw Arsenal fighting off speculation linking Cesc with a move to Barcelona. It was no secret that Barça and Real Madrid were big admirers of Fábregas' ability, but these latest reports left the midfielder bemused. His agent, Joseba Diaz, tried to set the record straight on the matter, but did little to ease the concern among Gunners fans: 'I have spoken with Cesc and we are not aware of any interest from Barça. And if they do have interest, hopefully they do because they are a great club, who play great football and Cesc was very happy there.'

Diaz also spread the news in Madrid-based Spanish magazine *Marca*, saying: 'What will come, will come. If we received an offer from Barcelona, clearly we would listen to it. It is the club which taught Cesc everything and it would be a compliment if that happened.' Fábregas, himself, remained quiet on the matter but, as a big Barcelona supporter, it was only natural that he would want to play for the Spanish giants one day. But he was happy at the Emirates. What's more, he had signed a contract with Arsenal, and the club expected him to honour that deal.

Fábregas simply focused on his football and linked up with his Spanish colleagues during the international break. Aragones finally restored Cesc to the starting line-up against Denmark in the latest Euro 2008 qualifier and the team's performance seemed to go up a notch as they won 3-1 away from home. It was a boost for the youngster who had been eager to pull on the Spanish shirt again after spending so much time on the bench in previous qualifiers. The three points pushed Spain closer to sealing a place at Euro 2008, but Sweden and surprise package Northern Ireland – who had both beaten Fábregas and company last year – were also chasing a spot at the tournament. These two nations were Spain's remaining opponents, so the race for Euro 2008 was destined to go to the wire. Four days later, Fábregas made a brief cameo as a substitute in a friendly against Finland. A 0-0 draw was hardly surprising considering the effort the Spaniards had put in at the weekend.

On 20 October, after a two-week break, the Gunners welcomed Bolton to the Emirates. Before kick-off Fábregas and Wenger received warm applause from the Arsenal supporters as they collected their player and manager of the month awards. It was a well-deserved honour for Cesc, who had masterminded his side's strong start to the season. September had been an exceptional month for him. Bolton proved stubborn opponents, but eventually, in the final half hour, Arsenal wore them down. First, Kolo Toure fired home a free-kick – after a foul on Fábregas – and then Rosicky made sure of the points late on.

The Gunners' superb start to the season inevitably led to comparisons with the 'Invincibles' – the 2003/04 side who went a whole league season unbeaten. Fábregas had only just arrived at the club when that streak began, but he had learned plenty from those players since. The 'Invincibles' had been ruthless, particularly away from home where they refused to be bullied. The 2007/08 team were displaying the same trait while playing the flowing, attacking football that made the 'Invincibles' so easy on the eye.

These comparisons brought a little pressure. After all, it would take some effort to match such achievements. It

181

was flattering for Cesc to be linked with that historic side, but he tried to shrug off the topic when speaking to the media: 'We don't want to listen to talk that we are 'Invincibles', because we have had a good run of results. We have to go for the big competitions and I would say that the Premier League is the hardest.' Considering all the negativity in the wake of Patrick Vieira's exit, Fábregas now appeared to be vindicating Arsène's decision. The Spaniard had proved tough enough to handle life in the Premiership.

The impressive sequence of results showed no signs of ending in midweek. If anything, the Gunners were looking sharper than ever. Slavia Prague were torn to shreds by a rampant Arsenal side on the way to an emphatic 7-0 win. Fábregas was back among the goals, scoring twice, and young Theo Walcott also bagged a brace. The gulf in class between the two sides was embarrassing at times. With three wins out of three, Wenger was pleased to see his side topping group H.

Back in domestic action, Liverpool provided the Gunners with their first big test of the season in late October. Everyone agreed that Arsenal, and Fábregas in particular, had begun well, but they had not yet faced one of the top sides. Liverpool, like the Gunners, were unbeaten in the Premiership and it promised to be a tense afternoon at Anfield. With van Persie sidelined, Wenger opted to play five in midfield and just Adebayor up front. The match began disappointingly as Steven Gerrard struck a firm free-kick past Almunia to give the home side the lead. From then on, though, Arsenal dominated. While they may not have created a hatful of chances, Fábregas took control of the midfield and Liverpool were forced to play like the away side as they retreated into their own half.

Cesc, along with Hleb, gradually began to find space in the final third, but time was against Arsenal. Liverpool were still leading as the game entered the final fifteen minutes. Sensing the Gunners' unbeaten run was in serious jeopardy, Fábregas emerged to make his latest vital contribution. Picked out cleverly by Hleb's pass, Cesc burst beyond the Liverpool back four and slotted the ball under the advancing Reina with ten minutes to go. Incidentally, his crucial strike against Tottenham had also come in the eightieth minute, underlining the tireless energy in Fábregas' game. Cesc raced over to the away fans and was clearly relieved to have made up for an earlier close-range miss. This Arsenal side had shown its never-say-die attitude again.

There was still time for Fábregas to pop up again in the Liverpool area, but this time his shot cruelly smashed against the post and rebounded to safety. The final whistle blew and the Gunners grudgingly accepted the 1-1 scoreline. Wenger seemed content when he spoke to the media after the game and Cesc knew that he had netted another hugely important goal for his side. He had already comfortably surpassed last year's tally. But Fábregas could not put his finger on why he was scoring with such ease this season after his struggles in past campaigns. He received a well-earned break in midweek as Arsène opted to field his youngsters again in the Carling Cup at Sheffield United, a game Arsenal won 3-0, with Eduardo grabbing a brace.

Cesc had seen his fair share of Manchester United already in his short career, but the clash between Arsenal and United at the Emirates the following weekend promised to be another classic. And this time, Cesc would take on an even more prominent role in the action. United were putting a shaky start to the season behind them. Draws with Reading and Portsmouth, followed by a 1-0 derby loss to Manchester City, had put Sir Alex Ferguson's side under intense scrutiny early on. Now, though, with Rooney, Ronaldo and Tevez striking up better understandings, the champions were back in contention. Arsenal could not afford to give up any ground when the two sides squared off on 3 November. The teams were level at the top, but Arsenal had a game in hand.

The expectations on Cesc's shoulders were cranked up a notch by glowing comments made by Emmanuel Adebayor in the build-up to the game. The Togo striker told the press: 'At the moment, Cesc is the best in the world. It's between him and Barcelona's Lionel Messi. He's a great player, too, but, for me, it's Cesc Fábregas. It's not just because he's my team-mate, but the way he plays. Absolutely fantastic.'

Fábregas himself made a couple of comments pre-match, which showed that although the Arsenal and United players seemingly do not particularly like each other, there is plenty of respect on both sides. Cesc said: 'I love the way they [United] play. They are a great side. I always watch them play and they are the only team I really like watching in England every week.' He spoke for a large section of the population who found the style of football employed by Chelsea and Liverpool to be far from riveting.

As is so often the case, the centre of midfield appeared

to be where the match would be won or lost as Fábregas and Flamini locked horns with Owen Hargreaves and Anderson – both summer signings. Anderson in particular had caught the eye, doing a superb job of deputising for the injured Paul Scholes. All four midfielders on show were tireless runners and the battle was guaranteed to mean a gruelling ninety minutes for all involved.

In an even first half, Fábregas struggled to find his usual rhythm as United swarmed around him in midfield. As a result, Arsenal could not break the visitors down and the creativity that had cut through the likes of Derby and Tottenham was sadly missing. Worse was to follow as the champions took the lead just before half-time. Gallas was credited with an own goal after he diverted Rooney's effort into the net.

The Gunners trudged off behind at the break, but Cesc knew there was still time for a fightback. Arsenal had trailed 1-0 against United last season yet had come back to win 2-1. Wenger roused the team during the fifteen-minute interval and Fábregas responded in an all-action second half. It took just three minutes for Arsenal to draw level and the scorer was none other than Cesc himself. A neat build-up gave Adebayor a good chance. Van der Sar smothered his effort, but the loose ball eventually found its way to Fábregas, who calmly slid it home to spark wild celebrations at the Emirates. It was the type of composure Wenger had mentioned to Cesc during the summer and this goal seemed to illustrate the youngster's improvements. As Fábregas admitted in *The Sunday Times*: 'Last year my body would have gone towards the floor and the ball would have gone into the stand.' This time, he had not panicked and his body shape had been perfect.

The momentum was now with the Gunners and Fábregas continued to burst forward. As the game entered the final ten minutes, both sides looked weary and it seemed as though 1-1 might be the final score. Yet the drama was only just beginning. A great run by Patrice Evra presented Ronaldo with a simple opportunity. He beat Almunia and United were eight minutes away from a massive victory on their travels.

But the Gunners would not throw in the towel. Cesc drove his colleagues forward in search of a late equaliser and a cross from the left sparked chaos in the United box. Eventually, the ball broke to Gallas, who lashed a smart strike goalwards. Van der Sar clawed the shot out, but the officials correctly ruled it had crossed the line. Arsenal were level again in what turned out to be the last meaningful kick of the game.

At the end of an exhausting afternoon, Fábregas could reflect proudly on his team's display and he joined in the celebratory post-match huddle. He felt that the Gunners had been the better side on the day, just as they had been a week earlier at Anfield. In the past, Wenger's side had been accused of lacking fighting spirit, but during the course of the previous fortnight they had dispelled that myth by standing up to two of their biggest rivals. In Premiership terms, they were still in the driving seat and the Gunners boss was a pleased man when he spoke to the media after the game 'Our character was tested twice. We are still in charge of the title race because we are top with a game in hand.'

It amused Fábregas that he was being hailed as a far

better footballer because of his goalscoring. He honestly felt that his performances had been as good as other seasons, but acknowledged that getting on the scoresheet caught people's attention more easily. From his point of view, he was simply converting more chances than in previous years and he found all the extra praise a little baffling.

After two draws from the last two games, Cesc was determined to get back to winning ways. But Wenger opted to rest his young Spaniard for the trip to face Slavia Prague in the Champions League. With the Gunners comfortably placed in Group H, Arsène felt the time was right to test some of the squad's fringe players. A 0-0 draw reflected the absence of Fábregas' creativity, but the point gained was enough to put Arsenal through to the second round of the competition. All that remained was to ensure that they topped the group.

While his team-mates made heavy weather of their fixture in Prague, Fábregas took the chance to head back to Barcelona along with Hleb, who had also been rested. Cesc has struck up many friendships during his time at Arsenal, but his bond with Hleb was particularly strong. They were on the same wavelength on and off the pitch and the duo travelled to Spain to watch Barcelona face Rangers in their Champions League tie. Wenger had given the trip his blessing and Fábregas was able to meet up with friends and family as well as make use of his Barça season ticket.

This break meant that Cesc was fresh for the trip to Reading on 12 November. Playing on a Monday night put more pressure on the Gunners because United had won at the weekend to go top of the table. For once,

Fábregas was not on the scoresheet, but Arsenal overpowered Reading 3-1 to reclaim top spot. Flamini scored his first goal of the season while the team's second, netted by Adebayor, finished off a beautiful passing move, with Cesc providing the key assist. The only low point that night for Fábregas was the yellow card he picked up in the second half – his fifth of the season, earning him a one-match ban.

The international break saw Cesc link up with his colleagues for the final two Euro 2008 qualifiers against Sweden and Northern Ireland. On 17 November, Fábregas helped Spain pick up a 3-0 victory over the Swedes in Madrid that guaranteed their place at the summer's showpiece. It was a special moment. Cesc played in a more advanced role on the night – more reminiscent of the position he played for Spain's youth teams – and was involved in the opening goal, flicking on Xavi's corner for defender Joan Capdevila to score. The Spaniards' passing was far too slick for their opponents and manager Luis Aragones was rewarded for selecting Fábregas, Xavi and Iniesta in the same line-up. With qualification confirmed, Cesc could look forward to an exciting summer in Austria and Switzerland. At the other end of the spectrum, England's chances were looking less promising as they made heavy weather of a routine qualifying group.

There was nothing at stake for Spain in their last group game, but they found the desire to beat Northern Ireland 1-0 in Las Palmas. Xavi grabbed the winner and Cesc came off at half-time. Aragones did not want to push the players too hard considering the meaningless nature of the match for the Spaniards. The defeat ended Northern Ireland's Euro 2008 dreams – Sweden would join Spain as the qualifiers from Group F. Fábregas looked at the group table and felt pleased that he and his team-mates had bounced back from their early wobbles to record a tally of twenty-eight points from their twelve games, winning eight and drawing one of their last nine qualifiers. Meanwhile, England failed to qualify.

Two weeks later, after the international fixtures, Arsenal picked up another three points. Wigan, who had just appointed Steve Bruce as their new manager, resisted for eighty-three minutes before Gallas and then Rosicky snatched crucial goals. Fábregas missed the game due to suspension and without his midfield probing the Gunners were clueless at times. So often, his team-mates were accustomed to looking for him when the game was tight and it was worrying for Wenger to see his side lacking a creative spark without the Spaniard. Still, the three points were very valuable, especially as United lost 1-0 at Bolton. If Arsenal won their game in hand, they could go six points clear at the top.

They had some Champions League business to attend to first as Sevilla still hoped to take away top spot in the group from the Gunners. Arsenal's 0-0 draw in Prague had given the Spaniards hope and Wenger only opted to leave out a couple of his first-team players. He did not dare to leave out Fábregas – this was an important game. But despite taking the lead, Cesc and company were outplayed by Sevilla, who scored twice in ten minutes to lead 2-1 at the break. In the second half, Fábregas was forced to limp off after suffering a hamstring injury. It had not been one of his better displays and it made the Gunners' task even harder. Kanoute eventually sealed the contest with a late penalty.

It had been a disappointing evening for Arsenal. Cesc was frustrated with his performance, but the bigger worry came with the injury he was now nursing. Wenger, meanwhile, had been sent off just before Fredi Kanoute's goal after an altercation with the fourth official. It was the Gunners' first loss of the season and there was plenty of bitterness in the Arsenal camp. Sevilla were now in the driving seat and, if the Spaniards beat Slavia Prague, Fábregas and his team-mates would have to accept second place in the group and the prospect of a much tougher second-round tie in their pursuit of the Champions League trophy.

Switching his attention to the international scene momentarily in late November, Cesc watched with interest as the 2010 World Cup qualifying groups were drawn. The tournament certainly seemed a long way off and Fábregas' sights were set on Euro 2008, but he was eager to see the outcome of the draw nonetheless. Aragones' men were placed in Group 5 and would face Turkey, Belgium, Bosnia and Herzegovina, Armenia and Estonia. It was a difficult group to judge. If the Turks were on song they might prove a serious threat, but otherwise it seemed like plain-sailing for the Spaniards. It was a mouth-watering prospect, even if the tournament was still a whole two-and-a-half years away. Elsewhere, England would again face Croatia – the team that had ended Steve McClaren's Euro 2008 hopes.

December began well for Arsenal, with a 2-1 win over Aston Villa, but the next couple of weeks highlighted the effect of Fábregas' enforced absence. His hamstring problem kept him out of the matches at Newcastle and Middlesbrough and, with van Persie also missing, the

Gunners collected just one point out of a possible six. Newcastle were fighting to save Sam Allardyce's job and surged back from a goal down against the Gunners to draw 1-1.

Worse followed at the weekend; Middlesbrough outfought a depleted Arsenal side to win 2-1. It made it two bleak trips to the North East in a matter of days. Fábregas was a frustrated spectator as he watched the team's good start fading and saw Manchester United gaining ground quickly. The Gunners were just a point ahead at the top and it was a worrying time for everyone associated with the club. Arsenal fans hoped Cesc would be returning to the line-up soon. Many more afternoons like the one at the Riverside Stadium would surely see United move into pole position.

With another massive game the following weekend against Chelsea, Fábregas worked as hard as he could to regain full fitness. In midweek, the Gunners overcame Steaua Bucharest 2-1 at the Emirates, but a victory for Sevilla meant the Spaniards finished first in the group; Arsenal second.

Attention then turned to the weekend and 16 December had long been billed as 'Grand Slam Sunday', as first United faced Liverpool, then the Gunners took on Chelsea. It promised to be a pivotal weekend in the title race, giving early indications of which teams would hold their nerve under pressure.

Arsenal received a major boost when Fábregas was passed fit for the match against the Blues. His energy and creativity would be vital in unlocking a stubborn Chelsea defence and he had really pushed himself to be ready for the important clash. As the players completed their final preparations before the game, news filtered through of United's 1-0 win at Anfield, courtesy of a Carlos Tevez goal. Whether they admitted it or not, this result put more pressure on the Gunners as they walked out in front of a noisy Emirates crowd.

Recent encounters between Arsenal and Chelsea had been fiery affairs and this proved to be no different. Tackles flew in, players swarmed around the referee and there was plenty of pushing and shoving. Fábregas was in the thick of the action and reacted furiously to a nasty challenge by Chelsea skipper John Terry. The whistle had already blown for a free-kick when Terry launched himself into the tackle. The Spaniard was looking unhappy about it. This led to more bitter arguing and Emmanuel Eboue was guilty of a bad challenge which resulted in Terry limping from the field.

This was a critical moment. Tal Ben Haim replaced Terry and, from that moment onwards, Chelsea never looked as composed. The decisive moment arrived just before half-time. Fábregas sent a corner into the Blues' penalty area, Petr Cech misjudged the flight of the ball and Gallas headed the Gunners into the lead. It was a rare error from Cech and it sent the home fans into wild celebrations. The Blues tried to fight back in the second half, creating several openings, one of which was badly missed by Shaun Wright-Phillips. Late on, Cesc and Ashley Cole looked like they might come to blows after the Spaniard fouled Cole from behind. Referee Alan Wiley calmed the situation and booked Fábregas. The cautions were totting up. Ten yellow cards would mean a two-match ban and he was getting dangerously close to that figure. Arsenal could do without losing him in the title run-in.

Wenger's side should have extended their advantage, but held on for a 1-0 victory and three vital points. It was their first win over Chelsea since early 2004. Cesc had managed to play the full ninety minutes on his return from injury and he joined in the celebrations with the supporters after the game. The Gunners were still top and this, after losing to Middlesbrough, was a key result.

Wenger was full of praise for the character shown by Fábregas and his team-mates: 'We lost our first game of the season last weekend and this was a mental test. The defence was outstanding. We came back against a big team and got the job done, so congratulations to the players.' The result had come as a huge boost for the Arsenal squad – they were back on track. However, Chelsea boss Avram Grant remained adamant that his side had deserved at least a point from the game.

It had been a physically and emotionally draining afternoon, but Cesc knew from experience that things would only get tougher as Christmas approached. Unlike other European leagues, which took a break during the festive period, the Premiership fixture list always became more congested as the year drew to an end.

CHAPTER 7
FIGHTING FOR THE TITLE

Few had expected Arsenal to be top of the Premiership table going into the Christmas period, but Cesc and his team-mates were enjoying proving people wrong. However, there was a long way to go and Fábregas refused to start thinking about silverware. It was far too early for that. But he was thrilled the Gunners were still involved in all four competitions.

Arsenal's youngsters impressed again in the Carling Cup – the competition that had given Cesc his earliest taste of first-team action – as they beat Blackburn 3-2 in extra-time. Fábregas, now such an important member of the side, did not feature as Wenger sought to keep his talisman fresh for the busy Christmas schedule.

Earlier in the month, Cesc had been glued to the television as the Euro 2008 groups were drawn in Lucerne, Switzerland. Fábregas hoped Spain would receive a favourable set of opponents, although any team that had reached the tournament would, of course, be a talented side. The Spaniards were drawn in Group D alongside holders Greece, Russia and Sweden. It was arguably the easiest of the four groups – certainly a lot easier than Group C, which contained World Cup holders Italy, along with France, Holland and Romania.

Cesc was happy enough with this outcome, feeling hopeful that Spain could progress to the quarter-finals without too many problems. Spain would begin their campaign against Russia on 10 June, followed by clashes with Sweden and Greece on 14 and 18 June respectively. It promised to be an action packed summer. Spain would be among the favourites to lift the trophy, especially after the generosity they had received from the group draw.

On 21 December, there was more suspense as the Champions League second-round draw took place in Nyon and everyone awaited the outcome eagerly. The news was not good – or at least it was not what Arsenal had hoped for. The Gunners were paired with reigning champions AC Milan – perhaps the toughest possible opponents. Wenger remained upbeat, telling the media: 'I believe we can do it if we play at our best. If you ask me do we have a chance to knock them out, then I say "yes". If you want to win the Champions League then you have to beat the biggest clubs.'

Fábregas felt exactly the same. He respected the ability in the AC Milan side, but was confident the Gunners could progress to the quarter-finals. It would certainly be an exciting tie and Cesc looked forward to pitting his wits against the likes of Kaka and Andrea Pirlo in the Italians' midfield. The contrasting playing styles made it an intriguing clash as the pace and movement in the

Arsenal ranks went up against the patient, wily approach of AC Milan.

A North London derby was next for the Premiership leaders. Since their last meeting in mid-September, Tottenham had replaced former boss Martin Jol with Spaniard Juande Ramos. Ramos had enjoyed success at Sevilla, who the Gunners had faced in the Champions League, and seemed to have an excellent pedigree. Spurs had begun to climb the table and it promised to be an interesting afternoon at the Emirates.

After a tight, goalless first half, the Gunners seized the initiative after the interval. Typically, Fábregas was at the heart of the action. Cesc's display had been a little below par in the opening period, but his clever backheel found Adebayor, who placed his shot past Paul Robinson to give Arsenal the lead. Tottenham did not surrender though. Instead, they stunned the Emirates crowd by first equalising through Dimitar Berbatov after sixty-six minutes and then winning a penalty for a foul by Toure on the Bulgarian striker.

With glory staring Spurs in the face, it all went horribly wrong. Robbie Keane saw his spot-kick saved by Almunia and shortly afterwards substitute Nicklas Bendtner headed the winner for the Gunners from Fábregas' pinpoint corner. Arsenal had been fortunate to escape with the three points, but many claimed it was the sign of champions – grinding out a victory without playing at their best. Tottenham would have to wait to end their jinx against the Gunners. Cesc, meanwhile, took heart from the two assists he had collected that afternoon. It was the perfect start to the busy Christmas weeks.

The only fear for Arsenal was that the team would come to expect too much from Fábregas. His team-mates were already becoming accustomed to looking to Cesc in critical moments and the only blip in the Gunners' season had come during Fábregas' enforced spell on the sidelines with his hamstring injury.

Against Portsmouth on Boxing Day, the Spaniard had a quiet game as Harry Redknapp's side frustrated Arsenal on the way to a deserved 0-0 draw. It stopped the Gunners from returning to the top of the table and cast a cloud over the festivities. United's victory earlier in the day gave them a one-point lead at the top. Fratton Park had so often been a lucky ground for Wenger, but on this occasion the home side had stood up to Arsenal.

Wenger offered little praise to Portsmouth after the match, but Fábregas knew that Redknapp's game plan had worked well. The midfield areas had been congested and it left little space for Cesc to work his magic. The likes of Papa Bouba Diop and Sulley Muntari put in tireless displays to protect the Pompey back four. This match was also noteworthy for Arsenal's failure to score. Such occasions had become so rare during Wenger's spell in charge and this was the first league match in which Fábregas and company had not found the net all season.

As always, the media waited with interest to see how Arsenal responded to losing leadership of the league. How much character was there in this young side? Initially, the signs did not look good and eager reporters were reaching for their notepads as the Gunners fell behind early on away to Everton on 29 December. Still trailing 1-0 at half-time, Fábregas was desperate to turn things around, but knew that patient build-up play was the key to getting back into the game.

The second half was all Arsenal and it emphatically answered any questions about the team's spirit and character. The awful first forty-five minutes were a distant memory as a brace from Eduardo put the Gunners ahead before the hour mark and Wenger looked far more relaxed in the technical area. But Bendtner did little to help the situation, receiving a second yellow card for a poor challenge on Andy Johnson and leaving his team-mates to protect their lead with ten men.

Fortunately for Arsenal, the touch and passing of Fábregas, among others, enabled the team to complete a comfortable victory. Substitute Adebayor made it 3-1 and the pressure was eased. There was still time, though, for Cesc to influence the action again. In the eighty-fourth minute, he was struck by the arm of fellow Spaniard Mikel Arteta, who was shown a red card. The Everton players were incensed by Fábregas' reaction, feeling he had exaggerated the contact, and this led to pushing and shoving as the Toffees' frustrations boiled over. When Cesc was booked shortly after, Wenger substituted the Spaniard to ensure he did not lose his temper in the dying moments. Arsène brought on Rosicky, who made it 4-1 shortly after.

Everton boss David Moyes showed his frustration after the game as he fumed about Bendtner's nasty tackle and questioned Fábregas' reaction to the supposed elbow from Arteta. With a heavy dose of sarcasm, Moyes said: 'I hope his jaw is OK. He went down as if it was broken.' Cesc felt aggrieved at these claims. He had always tried to play the game in the right spirit.

Manchester United had lost 2-1 at West Ham that afternoon, sparking a double celebration in the Arsenal dressing room. Fábregas was upset over the late fracas, but could only have been delighted with the team's second-half response. They had dominated midfield and Eduardo, who was looking like a very handy player, had taken his goals very well. The Gunners were top of the table once again.

The camaraderie between the Arsenal midfielders was a key reason for their success on the field. Cesc, Hleb, Flamini and Rosicky all enjoyed each other's company off the field and this was reflected in the way they worked so hard as a unit in matches and produced the type of passing football that the Gunners loved to play. It was noticeable that when addressing the media, each of the midfielders was quick to point out the others' qualities.

By his 2007/08 standards, Cesc was currently suffering a goal drought. He had not scored since the 2-2 draw with Manchester United at the start of November. But his passing and assists remained his main focus – and they could not be faulted. Next for Gunners was a home game against West Ham, conquerors of United just days earlier. Arsenal, though, had no such problems as they scored twice in the first twenty minutes to clinch a 2-0 win. Fábregas laid on the opening goal for Eduardo with a clever lofted pass and the Croatian did the rest. Adebayor then scored an excellent second to leave the Hammers too much to do. United also won and so the Gunners' lead at the top remained two points.

Cesc and his team-mates began their FA Cup campaign on 6 January away to Burnley. Fábregas loved the competition – it had given him his first winner's medal at Arsenal – but Wenger opted to rest the midfielder after the hectic Christmas fixture list. Instead, Arsène gave Brazilians Gilberto Silva and Denilson the chance to impress in the centre of the pitch. Eduardo continued his hot streak with a goal in the ninth minute and Bendtner sealed the points with fifteen minutes to go. Cesc put his feet up and was happy to see the team progress to the fourth round.

Fábregas received more time off as Wenger continued to use his youngsters and fringe players in the Carling Cup. Tottenham were the opponents for the two-legged semi-final and were desperate to impress under new boss Ramos. The first leg finished 1-1, with Spurs the better side. Arsène must have wondered how different things might have been had he included Cesc and other first-team players in the squad. It would be a big night at White Hart Lane in two weeks' time and Spurs had a slight advantage.

Fábregas was finally back in action on 12 January as Arsenal entertained Birmingham at the Emirates. He had not played since New Year's Day and felt fresh going into the game. David Beckham – who was training with the Gunners during the close season of the American MLS – was among those watching, but Cesc and company endured a disappointing afternoon. Adebayor gave the Gunners the lead, but Birmingham pulled level just after the interval and successfully shut the door on subsequent Arsenal attacks.

Fábregas did his best to influence the game: shooting from distance, playing through balls for Adebayor and Eduardo. But it was just not their day; perhaps they were missing Kolo Toure who, along with Eboue, had left to represent the Ivory Coast at the African Cup of Nations. Cesc left the field irritated that the side had dropped valuable points. To make matters worse, United later won 6-0 at home to Newcastle, with Ronaldo grabbing his first hat-trick for the club. The Red Devils leapfrogged Arsenal into top spot.

It was a long week for Fábregas as he impatiently waited to make amends for the draw with Birmingham. Saturday finally came and the Gunners were away at Fulham, who had appointed Roy Hodgson to replace Lawrie Sanchez. With United away at Reading, all eyes were on the country's top two sides. Arsenal made no mistake, taking the game by the scruff of the neck to lead 2-0 at half-time, with both goals coming courtesy of Adebayor headers. Fábregas almost made it 3-0 in the second half, but his effort narrowly missed the target. Rosicky succeeded where Cesc had failed, however, netting late on to cap a superb display. Such was the Gunners' dominance, Wenger opted not to make a single substitution. United sneaked a 2-0 win at Reading, but the Gunners were staying right on the tails of Ferguson's side and looked ready to take the title race right to the wire.

Having missed the Carling Cup semi-final first leg against Tottenham, Cesc was pleased to be included in the squad for the return match as Arsène decided to use more of his first-team players. Wenger was obviously concerned by the quality Spurs had shown in the first leg. Fábregas started the game on the bench, but an injury to Denilson after just eighteen minutes saw Cesc enter the action sooner than he could possibly have imagined. Tottenham were already a goal up and the atmosphere inside White Hart Lane was electric. Things went from bad to worse for Fábregas and the Gunners as Spurs found themselves 4-0 up after just an hour.

It was not one of Cesc's better performances. There were more misplaced passes than usual and he could never settle into a rhythm. Adebayor, also on as a substitute, pulled a goal back, but there was no chance of a comeback. In fact, it was Tottenham who scored again as Steed Malbranque made it 5-1. The most disappointing moment came late on, though, with an incident involving Bendtner and Adebayor, before captain Gallas stepped in to calm the situation. Arsenal had been well and truly rattled and Wenger would have to discipline the warring duo. Ten days after the draw with Birmingham, Fábregas again found himself trudging off at the final whistle with his head hung in dismay. It had been a night to forget for all Gunners fans – Spurs supporters would be unbearable in the wake of this scoreline.

There was little time to dwell on this setback, though, as an FA Cup fourth-round tie with Newcastle awaited at the weekend. The Magpies had recently sacked Sam Allardyce and then stunned the world with the appointment of former boss Kevin Keegan as his replacement. The media were highly critical, but many Newcastle fans were delighted and the positive mood on Tyneside made the tie trickier for Fábregas and his team-mates.

Yet the Gunners were not feeling sentimental and Keegan did not register the morale-boosting win he was hoping for. Fábregas worked hard in midfield as Arsenal secured a 3-0 victory and a place in the fifth-round draw. Adebayor netted twice and a Nicky Butt own goal completed the scoring from Cesc's free-kick. Wenger was pleased and hoped for another home tie when the draw was made on the Monday.

United, Chelsea and Liverpool all won their games and Fábregas was keen to avoid the fellow big boys until the later stages of the competition. Incredibly, though, fate had other ideas and the draw paired the Gunners with Manchester United – easily the biggest clash of the round. Nonetheless, Cesc was excited to pit his wits against United again. The BBC quickly pounced on the rights for the fixture and the countdown to the match began.

Fábregas lined up against Newcastle again in midweek as the two sides squared off in Premiership action this time. The crowd at the Emirates looked on expectantly, praying for a repeat of Arsenal's FA Cup victory. Keegan, meanwhile, was still seeking a first win and a first goal since starting his second stint as Magpies boss.

Cesc had spoken out prior to the game about the Gunners keeping their focus and concentrating on their own performances. He told the media: 'All we know is that we have to keep winning. We do not have to look at the others, we have to look at ourselves – if we win every game, we will be champions.' The players responded well to Fábregas' comments and collected their second 3-0 win over Newcastle in the space of four days. Cesc got back among the goals too, scoring the third to cap a strong midfield display. Earlier, Adebayor had grabbed the first before Flamini smashed a brilliant second.

After the game, Fábregas had nothing but praise for

Adebayor, telling the press: 'Emmanuel is one of the best in the world, without any doubt. You cannot fault him in any way. He works, he defends, he chases the centre-backs, he goes behind, he can play to feet, he has a good first touch and a good technique. He has improved amazingly and I don't think we could live without Adebayor right now.' It was a ringing endorsement for the Togo front man and everyone at the club was relieved that the striker was not in African Cup of Nations action.

Cesc also reserved kind words for Flamini: 'Mathieu has been amazing all season. He is hyperactive, on the pitch, outside the pitch. He has so much passion for the game. He hates losing. With his encouragement, we play better.' The Gunners went top of the table temporarily, only for United to return to the summit the next day with a comfortable, Ronaldo-inspired 2-0 victory over Portsmouth.

The latest news from Real Madrid was that they had given up hope of capturing Fábregas' signature. Cesc and Cristiano Ronaldo had been at the top of their wishlist for some time, but Arsenal and United had shown equal resolve in hanging onto their young stars. Fábregas hoped the saga would die down now that Real had accepted his decision to stay at the Emirates. At least his mother, Nuria, had not followed the example set by Ronaldo's mother, who publicly urged her son to sign for the Spanish giants.

The Gunners had the chance to return to the top at the weekend as they faced Manchester City in Saturday's early kick-off. Trips to the City of Manchester Stadium had not ended well for visiting teams this season and

Fábregas knew it would be a tough afternoon. City boss Eriksson had built an exciting side and Cesc remembered how close the match between the two clubs at the Emirates had been.

On the day, though, Arsenal were just too good as Adebayor continued his fine run of form. Led by Fábregas, the Gunners played some beautiful football on the way to a 3-1 victory. Cesc was heavily involved in the third goal, surging forward and laying the ball into the path of Adebayor, who made no mistake. United could only draw 1-1 at Tottenham, so Wenger's side returned to the top.

Reflecting on how the season was panning out, Fábregas told the press: 'Even though we are still young, we have shown the world what we can do. We have had to learn to be patient, and now we have taken our chance. We would be very disappointed if we didn't win it [the title]. That's certain.' Cesc, though, dismissed suggestions that it was simply a race between Arsenal and United, pointing out that Chelsea were only six points behind the Gunners and four behind Ferguson's team: 'There's not only Manchester United, there's also Chelsea. We'll see what happens, but I'm sure they'll be there at the end.'

Despite all the negative comments surrounding Avram Grant's appointment as Jose Mourinho's replacement, the new boss had done a good job at Stamford Bridge without injured stars Terry, Drogba and Lampard. The Blues still had home fixtures against Arsenal, United and Liverpool and so it was impossible to rule them out of the title race. Benitez's side, meanwhile, acknowledged that fourth place was the best they could realistically aim for.

Fábregas linked up with his international colleagues for a friendly against France in Malaga on 6 February. Though publicly the talk of revenge for the World Cup defeat was dismissed, Cesc and his team-mates wanted to make amends for that loss by putting one over on the French. The youngster began the match on the bench, but came on with the score goalless and helped his colleagues achieve a 1-0 victory. Admittedly, there were no points at stake, but any win over a team of France's calibre was a good result and Fábregas felt that Spain had put together some lovely passing moves, though they were fortunate to hold off late French pressure.

After jetting back from Malaga, Cesc focused on Arsenal again and their bid for silverware. Next for the Gunners was a home game against Blackburn – a side who had caused a few upsets against Arsenal in the past. Fábregas recalled his spat with Rovers boss Mark Hughes during the previous season and knew that Blackburn would be fired up. Wenger had several selection worries as he waited on the fitness of Flamini and tried to arrange for Toure to return from the African Cup of Nations in time for the clash with Rovers.

It was a Monday night fixture and so Cesc and his team-mates had already received the boost of seeing United lose a Manchester derby (made emotional by the fiftieth anniversary of the Munich air disaster) on the Sunday afternoon. It was a loss few could have expected, considering United's imperious home form, but it came as welcome news in North London as it meant Arsenal could stretch their lead to five points at the top with a victory.

Prior to the Rovers game, Wenger told the media how

impressed he was with the maturity his team were showing, particularly Fábregas: 'They are all more mature now. Cesc is committed and you always like your players to have a winning attitude. Sometimes it can go a little bit over the top, but Cesc has behaved remarkably well this season – I cannot remember one incident. There was maybe a stage six months ago, where he went a bit the wrong way – but he corrected that very well, without any special management from me. He apologised and from then on there have been no problems with him. He is so intelligent he realised that is not the way he wanted to go.' It was apt timing for this discussion as it was against Rovers that the midfielder had had his most public tantrum.

It was true. Fábregas had curbed his temper and had made a point of cutting out his tantrums. Now that he held such a key role within the side, he knew he had to act more responsibly and set an example for his team-mates. There was no doubt the weekend's results had gone the Gunners' way – with United losing and Chelsea drawing 0-0 with Liverpool at Stamford Bridge. Now Cesc and his colleagues had to cash in.

Predictably, Arsenal came out strongly against Blackburn, as though they were eager to send a message to United. Senderos scored from a corner within four minutes and it looked like Fábregas – who was playing on the right of midfield – and his colleagues would go on to secure an easy win. Yet Blackburn made life tough and created several decent chances. Cesc worked hard to get involved in attacks from out wide and was given licence to roam infield. His clever header released Flamini, whose shot was well saved by Brad Friedel in the Rovers goal. Adebayor finally sealed the win in stoppage time. The only low point on the night was a booking for Fábregas that took his tally for the season to nine – one more caution would bring a two-match suspension. Wenger could do without losing Cesc with so many key games ahead.

The Arsenal players formed their customary post-match huddle and celebrated their five-point lead at the top of the table. It had been a superb few days for the club. Wenger praised his players, but remained cautious: 'We are in a good position. We believe we can do it. But there's still a long way to go. It's far from being over. As soon as you're not at your best at the top, you can drop points. We'll have to fight until the last minute of the championship.'

Meanwhile, the football results in Spain were not so pleasing for Fábregas. His beloved Barcelona were faltering badly as they sought to recapture the La Liga title. Worse still, champions and deadly rivals Real Madrid were the side leaving Barça trailing in their wake. As a big Barcelona fan, Cesc found it hard to take: the league table did not make for good reading. Real had established an eight-point lead – just a day before Arsenal had stretched their own advantage to five points at the top of the Premiership. Fábregas' good friend Messi was in fine form, but others were struggling badly and the Spanish press were putting the team under extra pressure. It was a disappointment for Cesc that Barcelona were not emulating the Gunners' super form.

Fábregas was in the headlines again on 15 February when news of a contract extension offer from Arsenal reached the media. Andrew Dillon of the *Sun* was quick to latch onto the story, writing: 'Cesc Fábregas will rocket to the top of Arsenal's pay league – with an amazing new deal worth £33 million. Gunners manager Arsène Wenger wants the Spanish midfielder, twenty, to commit until 2016 by signing a two-year extension to his current contract.' The newspaper also speculated as to Fábregas' pay increase, suggesting that the player's wage might jump from £50,000 a week to £80,000. It showed how valuable the Spaniard had become to the club. Wenger and the Arsenal hierarchy were deeply concerned that Cesc might be snatched away and wanted to tie him down to a longer contract. As always, Fábregas was highly diplomatic when discussing interest from Barcelona: 'I am proud to be linked to Barcelona. I am from the city and have played there. But now I only think of Arsenal.'

The following weekend saw the Gunners in FA Cup action again as the big games kept coming. And it did not get much bigger than Manchester United away. With both sides eyeing up a possible Treble, this tie would end the dream for one of them. Fábregas had good memories of his last trip to Old Trafford when his run and through ball had set up Adebayor's late winner. Another 1-0 victory would be most welcome. But Cesc was aware that United would be like a wounded animal after the defeat to City and that they would be more fired up than ever, especially with psychological points on offer for the title race.

The United-Arsenal clash was by far the most intriguing of the round. An easier tie would have allowed Wenger and Ferguson to rest players ahead of European commitments, but neither was willing to field heavily weakened sides for such a significant match. Fábregas always looked forward to big occasions at spectacular venues and the trip to Old Trafford was no different. The Theatre of Dreams was just that for the Spaniard and he hoped it would be the scene of another vital Arsenal victory. Cesc returned to his usual central midfield berth and the Gunners welcomed Toure back into the defence. United, meanwhile, were strengthened by the return of Rooney and Evra from suspension.

Nobody could have predicted the way that the game would pan out, though. Fábregas and his team-mates never got going and Ferguson's side gave them a 4-0 hammering – and it could, and should, have been more. The Spaniard put in one of his worst performances of the season as United looked the hungrier side. Loose balls in midfield were seized upon by the men in red and for the second time that season the Brazilian Anderson did an effective job of overshadowing Cesc in their midfield duel.

Two goals from Darren Fletcher and further strikes from Rooney and Nani completed a miserable afternoon in Manchester that brought back memories of Arsenal's 6-1 capitulation to United in 2001. Eboue was red-carded in the second half as the Gunners showed their nasty side with further petulant fouling from Hoyte and Gallas among others. The Arsenal skipper was lucky not to be sent off. Fábregas was substituted by Wenger with twenty minutes to go. The game was already over as a contest and Arsène wanted the Spaniard to be as fresh as possible for the visit of AC Milan in midweek.

The Arsenal manager denied suggestions that his players had not been as motivated by FA Cup glory and said: 'It was an off day. It just didn't work for us today. We were beaten everywhere and we never looked like coming back.' Wenger also refused to criticise his players for their aggressive approach in the second half. Having complained so much about United's physicality in previous meetings, the Gunners could expect little sympathy after these antics.

Arsenal certainly did not escape criticism in the media the next day as reporters condemned their lacklustre efforts. Statistics in the *Observer* pointed out that Wenger's side did not have a shot on target during the entire ninety minutes and reporter Kevin Mitchell blasted them, writing: 'Napoleon can hardly have retreated from Moscow with less dignity than Arsenal returned to London from Manchester. This drubbing exposed not only the team's inadequacy on the day, but also Wenger's tepid commitment to the FA Cup.'

The *Daily Express* was also critical of the Gunners' careless passing and credited United for their first-class display. Worse was to follow in the *Independent* on Monday when columnist James Lawton slammed the attitude of the Arsenal team in a piece bemoaning the big teams' lack of interest in the FA Cup. Lawton wrote: 'What was so gut-wrenching here was not just the performance but the demeanour of the team that leads the Premier League by five points. The performance was putrid. The demeanour was sickening.' Newspaper reports from this match did not even mention Fábregas' contribution – one of the few times this season that his name had not cropped up in articles.

The Spaniard was well aware that he and his team-mates had to be careful that their season did not slide downhill. He recalled how Arsenal had lost out in the Carling Cup final the previous season and had followed that with FA Cup and Champions League exits in quick succession. Cesc knew the whole complexion of a season could change dramatically in a matter of weeks. Now the Gunners were out of both domestic cup competitions and the players were under more pressure to win the Premiership and the Champions League.

Fábregas was keen to put the below-par display at Old Trafford behind him and luckily he had the perfect distraction in midweek as all attention naturally turned to the Champions League. The Gunners' second-round opponents, AC Milan, had enjoyed a strong two months domestically after a terrible start to the league campaign and were finally clawing their way back towards the top four in Serie A.

Fábregas knew the Italian giants were a different animal in Europe as, regardless of their league form, Milan always put on a show in the Champions League. But Cesc and his team-mates were in great shape themselves. The five-point lead in the Premiership eased some of the pressure and the spirit within the side was there for all to see. It promised to be a fascinating duel as Arsenal squared off against the reigning European champions.

While most of the talk surrounding AC Milan revolved around Brazilian star Kaka and youthful compatriot Alexandre Pato, those who watched them regularly knew that it was the midfield areas which would be pivotal to the outcome of the tie. Fábregas, Flamini, Hleb and Rosicky seemed the likeliest quartet for the Gunners and they would have to match the intensity of Milan midfielders Massimo Ambrosini and Gennaro Gattuso. Most importantly, though, Cesc needed to get close to Andrea Pirlo, the deep-lying Italian playmaker. Pirlo's effortless passing and calm temperament had been the driving force behind many of the club's triumphs and anyone who watched the 2006 World Cup would have noticed the effect he had on his team-mates. If Fábregas could win the battle with Pirlo, Arsenal would surely stand an excellent chance of progressing to the quarter-finals.

It would certainly be a battle pitting the young against the old. The Milan side still contained the likes of Paolo Maldini, a few months short of his fortieth birthday – who made his Serie A debut two years before Cesc was born and made his 1,000th Milan appearance at the weekend before the first leg – and, for all their experience, they were vulnerable to the pace and movement of youthful opponents. When the draw was made, Wenger had been positive about Arsenal's chances and he remained optimistic in the build-up to the game. Brazilian striker Ronaldo had been ruled out for the Italian giants with a knee injury – picked up a week before – and AC Milan did not look as deadly up front without him, especially as Kaka and Pato were also going into the game carrying injuries.

Playing the first leg at home had its advantages and disadvantages. While Fábregas would doubtless have preferred to have the Emirates crowd behind the Gunners in the return match, Arsenal had the chance to put the tie to bed in the first leg, or at least give themselves breathing space for the trip to Milan. That could be pivotal to the team's chances.

As usual, Fábregas was sought out by the media pre-match for his verdict on the game and Arsenal's chances of victory. Cesc explained: 'Milan are maybe not doing too well in Serie A, but they are different in the Champions League. They have one of the strongest midfields in the world. We all know that Italian teams know how to play these kinds of games, but we're not scared of anything. We respect them a lot because they are a great side with great players who have won nearly everything. We want to be like them one day and this is one of the days where you can show you are ready for a big future.'

Fábregas added that the loss to United would not be weighing on his mind: 'Yes, the 4-0 was difficult to understand. I felt very bad. But the players will bounce back.' Heads might have been down for a couple of days, but not any more. The glamour of the Champions League was enough to get any footballer excited.

The Milan camp appeared to be quietly confident. Manager Carlo Ancelotti insisted that a defeat at the Emirates would not be irreversible and Kaka neglected to mention Arsenal when he ran through a list of favourites for the competition. Captain Maldini offered a more honest assessment of the Italians' mood: 'This team [Arsenal] has been growing, and it'll be a lot harder facing them now than it was in the past.' No doubt, Fábregas would be a marked man in midfield as Milan were expected to crowd the central areas. The tireless Ambrosini would probably try to stick tight to Cesc all night.

The clashes at the Emirates against Manchester United and Chelsea had been serious tests of how far the

Gunners had come and the team had passed muster on both occasions. The visit of AC Milan, though, promised to be their biggest yet. Wenger agreed, claiming that the tie with Milan was 'the ultimate test' of how soon his squad would be ready to reach the top in Europe. As the teams walked out in front of a packed crowd on 20 February, there was a feeling of expectation in the air. Cesc needed no reminding just how massive a night it was for the club and was eager to leave his mark on the contest. Ideally, he wanted the Gunners to have a comfortable lead to take to Milan for the return game.

But it was a night of frustration for the home side as the Italians rode their luck on the way to producing a resolute defensive display as the Gunners lacked a clinical touch in front of goal. The first leg ended 0-0, but Fábregas knew that Arsenal should have scored at least a couple of goals. Milan, led superbly by the brilliant Maldini, worked hard to deny Cesc and company space, but several lightning moves gave the Gunners scoring opportunities. Eboue missed a decent opening, Fábregas twice forced saves from goalkeeper Zeljko Kalac and then Adebayor squandered the best chance of the night, heading against the bar from just yards out.

The visitors had offered little threat themselves and Cesc told the media post-match that the Arsenal players were disappointed not to have won, but still remained confident of finishing the job in Italy: 'After a big defeat against Manchester United at the weekend we came back strong. We had quite a lot of chances, but in football you have to take them. Hopefully, we won't regret it and we can go there, play the same way and I am sure we can win. If we can score a goal I think we have a good opportunity to go through.' On a personal level, Fábregas could have done no more on the night to help break the deadlock.

Wenger added: 'I think it was a very good game. We have shown a maturity and we kept a clean sheet, which is very positive for the second leg. We were completely dominant for the whole of the second half, but we couldn't take advantage with a goal. I felt the impact we got on them today though will certainly have a part to play in the second game and I'm very happy with the response I got today from my team.'

It set things up beautifully for the second leg in the San Siro. Milan would be favourites, considering their home advantage, but if Arsenal could score an away goal in Italy, the complexion of the tie would alter dramatically. Fábregas was encouraged by the style of the Gunners' display at the Emirates and he had enjoyed a magnificent game himself, controlling everything in midfield. Meanwhile, the other English teams had fared relatively well. Chelsea and Manchester United both drew the away legs of their ties while Liverpool picked up a morale boosting 2-0 victory over Inter Milan at Anfield.

With the Gunners failing to take their chances against Milan, there was a slight anxiety over the side's current form. There were only two competitions left to play for and Fábregas and his team-mates needed to go the distance in both to do themselves justice. The hard work was only just beginning. He did not want to look back at the end of the season with regrets over what might have been. There would be no excuses for failure.

Cesc hoped there would be no hangover from the midweek exertions when they faced Birmingham at St

Andrews in Saturday's early kick-off. The players had given every ounce of energy against AC Milan, but Fábregas would not accept that excuse if Arsenal dropped points. This was the business end of the season and he expected to be giving 110 percent week in, week out as the team chased domestic and European glory.

Fábregas and his team-mates were determined to come flying out of the traps against Birmingham and extend their lead at the top to eight points before United took on Newcastle later that day. There were murmurs in the media suggesting that the Gunners were stuttering and Cesc was keen to put the record straight. He would let his football do the talking.

But there was a soul-destroying moment ahead for all those connected with Arsenal. Just minutes into the clash with Birmingham, Eduardo suffered a bad challenge by defender Martin Taylor that left his leg horrifically shattered. As Fábregas and his team-mates looked on in dismay, the striker was stretchered from the field after lengthy treatment. Taylor was sent off for the tackle, but it was the Gunners who suffered more from the incident. Cesc and company were noticeably shaken to see their friend in such pain and they struggled to find their usual form. The Spaniard in particular appeared badly affected by Eduardo's discomfort.

James McFadden gave the home side the lead, but a Walcott brace looked to have clinched the points for Arsenal. However, there was another twist as Birmingham managed to snatch a 2-2 draw after Clichy conceded a late penalty. It sparked several minutes of mayhem as Gallas ranted at Clichy and then stormed up to the other end of the pitch and sat down. McFadden scored from the spot and Wenger had to coax Gallas into leaving the pitch at the final whistle. It was undoubtedly Arsenal's least memorable weekend of the season and Fábregas was still in shock as he trudged off.

Wenger heaped criticism on Taylor after the game for the tackle that looked set to keep Eduardo on the sidelines for up to a year. The Frenchman said: 'This tackle was horrendous and this guy [Taylor] should never play football again.' Wenger later admitted that his comments were over the top, but his outburst suggested that the Arsenal dressing room was beginning to feel the heat in the title race. Above all, though, the injury to Eduardo reminded Fábregas of how fragile a career in sport could be and how important it was to savour every minute. United's 5-1 demolition of Newcastle completed a miserable day for the Gunners as their lead was cut to three points. Unfortunately for Cesc, on the domestic front at least, things would not be getting better in a hurry.

The next weekend, the gap was reduced to a single point as Arsenal could only draw at home to Aston Villa while United won with ease at Fulham. In truth, it could have been worse for Fábregas as the Gunners needed a late equaliser to salvage their draw. Cesc wasted one very good opportunity as the team failed to shake off the gloom surrounding Eduardo's injury. Meanwhile, United looked fresh and were in sensational form.

As the Gunners prepared to fly over to Milan for the massive second leg, nobody needed to remind Fábregas that Arsenal would have to find a better performance in midweek. No English team had won in the San Siro and United had been decimated there in the previous season's semi-final. However, Cesc made it clear before the game that this Gunners side feared no one and would look to play as expansively as usual. Apart from an injury to Clarence Seedorf, Milan were able to unleash all their big guns as they looked to push towards the latter stages of a competition they will always be associated with.

The match was, in many ways, a carbon copy of the first leg. After a nervy start, Arsenal dominated possession with Fábregas and Hleb heavily involved in some beautiful passing moves. Meanwhile, the Italians were content to soak up the pressure and wait for their chance to strike. But it never came as the Gunners produced their most impressive display of the campaign.

Such was Arsenal's superiority it was easy to forget that AC Milan were the reigning champions. Adebayor was always dangerous, while Senderos and Eboue also had good chances in front of goal. To add to the frustration, referee Konrad Plautz denied the visitors a clear free-kick on the edge of the area and incredibly booked Hleb for diving instead. For the champions, Kaka gave brief glimpses of his talent, but was well shackled by Cesc and Flamini while Inzaghi and Pato rarely worried Gallas and Toure.

With just over five minutes remaining, it looked as though Milan had once again survived the Arsenal onslaught and both managers must have begun to consider extra-time. Yet Fábregas had no such thoughts. His tireless style of play ensures that he is just as likely to punish opponents in the first minute as he is in the last and, in the eighty-fourth minute, he stepped forward to deliver his latest vital contribution. He had inspired the Gunners many times during the season, but this was certainly his biggest moment.

Picking the ball up inside the Milan half, Cesc drove towards goal as defenders backed away. With limited support, he opted to shoot from distance and sent a skidding 30-yard shot beyond Kalac's dive and into the bottom corner. You could hear a pin drop in the San Siro as Fábregas, arms outstretched, raced off to celebrate. There was no way back for Milan. Arsenal were going through to the quarter-finals. Adebayor added a second for good measure, but it was Cesc who would steal the headlines. On a night when so much had been expected from World Player of the Year Kaka, it was Fábregas who had been the hero.

The Spaniard was overwhelmed as he spoke to the media after the match: 'This is a dream come true. But this is just the beginning. We are now in the quarter-finals, but we have not done anything. It is just one more step.' Wenger, meanwhile, could not have been prouder of the performance.

Back in Premiership action, though, Arsenal continued to falter. A 0-0 draw away to Wigan was followed by a 1-1 deadlock at home to Middlesbrough. Pundits questioned whether the players were still struggling to shrug off the memories of the Eduardo injury. Meanwhile, United took full advantage and their victory over Bolton on 19 March put them three points ahead of the Gunners. Ronaldo was in electrifying form and, with Adebayor suffering a goal drought, seemed a certainty to pick up the Golden Boot at the end of the campaign.

Fábregas could not explain how Arsenal's title challenge had slipped away. The European exertions had certainly taken their toll on the players, but Cesc refused to use this as an excuse. Though the win in Milan had been an incredible night, it was in the past now. He eagerly awaited the quarter-final draw but, when it came, it was not the news the Gunners were hoping for. They would face Liverpool, experts in that competition. It would be a tough tie, but Fábregas fancied Arsenal's chances against anyone.

Wenger, like Cesc, had wanted to avoid a fellow English side but remained positive, telling the media: 'I said ideally you would like to play a foreign team because it's Europe, but I prepared myself to play anyone. We are highly determined to go through.' The other significant news from the Champions League draw was the set-up for the semi-finals. The winner of the Arsenal-Liverpool quarter-final would take on either Chelsea or Turkish side Fenerbahce while the winner between Manchester United and Roma would face Barcelona or Schalke. As Fábregas instantly noticed, the Gunners could face Premiership opponents in the next two rounds as well if they progressed that far.

The following weekend was the second coming of Grand Slam Sunday, but it came at the wrong time for the out-of-sorts Arsenal players. The Gunners had got the better of Chelsea in December while United had overcome Liverpool. Now they would have to do it all again. At Old Trafford, Ferguson's side kept up their end of the bargain, winning 3-0 against Liverpool and heaping pressure on both Arsenal and Chelsea.

Cesc knew that United would be watching the Chelsea-Arsenal clash keenly, but refused to lose his nerve. He had played in enough big games already in his short career to know how to handle such an occasion. The Spaniard was well aware that four consecutive draws in the league was unacceptable, but felt that the Gunners were just one good result away from turning things around.

After a tight first half at Stamford Bridge, Fábregas and his team-mates took the lead just before the hour mark. Cesc's inch-perfect corner was headed home by Sagna. It looked as though Arsenal might end their rotten Premiership run with a massive three points. But Chelsea had title intentions of their own and, in Drogba, had a striker capable of turning the game on its head. The Ivorian scored twice in nine minutes to leave the Gunners floored. It was very quiet in the Arsenal dressing room after the game as their worrying predicament began to sink in.

Arsenal suddenly found themselves six points behind United and one behind Chelsea who were now second. How had it all gone wrong in the space of a few weeks? Wenger tried to remain positive when he spoke to the media: 'We will fight until the end and we are not worried about the future but are disappointed now, obviously. Today we were unlucky and I thought we played well.' Fábregas' title dreams were in tatters and he knew that four points out of a possible fifteen was not good enough.

Confidence within the side had been visibly shaken by the poor run of results and a trip to Bolton the following Saturday was the last thing Arsenal needed. Initial worries were confirmed as the Gunners found themselves trailing 2-0 at half-time and down to ten men after Diaby's dismissal. However, at last the character of the Arsenal side shone through. To his credit, Fábregas bounced back from a poor first half to help lead the charge. Goals from Gallas and van Persie – from the penalty spot – made it 2-2 before Cesc burst onto Hleb's cut-back and saw his shot deflected into the net for a late winner.

Even the normally calm Wenger was on his feet celebrating as the rain continued to pour. The Gunners were still in the title race. The mood was dampened slightly by United's 4-0 victory over Aston Villa later in the day, but Fábregas was delighted nonetheless with the team's spirited comeback.

Wenger told the media: 'I am very proud of our performance. The first half we didn't play badly, but everything went against us. We did absolutely everything to win the game and we got a very important victory for us.' With three huge clashes with Liverpool on the horizon, the Gunners had shown they were not running out of steam. Fábregas knew that the next few weeks would make or break Arsenal's season and he was determined to make big contributions – just as he had in the San Siro.

Also, there was still a huge game at Old Trafford against Manchester United for Fábregas and his team-mates to gain ground on the leaders. It would be an opportunity for Arsenal to avenge the 4-0 defeat in the FA Cup when the Gunners had woefully underperformed against such fierce rivals. It was the type of match that always seemed to bring out the best in Cesc.

However, disappointment was just around the corner. April was always going to be a tricky month for Fábregas and Arsenal, but it certainly did not go according to plan as the club exited the Champions League and saw their title chances fade away.

Wenger's youngsters, and the influential Fábregas in particular, were finally showing signs of fatigue after setting the football world alight for so much of the season. Could Cesc lift his team-mates?

The month started with three games against rivals Liverpool, the two legs of the Champions League quarter-final separated by a home Premiership fixture. The Champions League home tie came first and was a thoroughly frustrating experience for Fábregas and company. Despite the Spaniard playing a part in Adebayor's 23rd-minute opener, Arsenal were unable to hold on to the lead and had to settle for a 1-1 draw, though Fábregas went close with a late header. The result made Liverpool favourites to go through with their all-important away goal.

However, Fábregas and his team-mates had no time to dwell on their failings. Liverpool were their opponents again three days later, this time in the Premiership. Again the outcome was 1-1. This time, a Crouch strike was cancelled out by a Bendtner header from yet another Fábregas free-kick. The goals may have dried up for the Spaniard, but the vital assists certainly had not. A draw was certainly not the result that the Gunners were looking for at the Emirates Stadium but it did not rule them out of the title race just yet. They would have to step up a few gears though if they wanted to save their Premiership bid.

Fábregas was in action again three days later for his third game in less than a week. Exhaustion was certainly catching up with the Spaniard as he was unable to prevent Arsenal from crashing out of the Champions League with a 4-2 defeat to Liverpool at Anfield.

Arsenal's general tiredness was clear for all to see as

they were undone by late goals by Gerrard – from the penalty spot – and Babel. One trophy gone, but one still just about possible for Fábregas and Arsenal.

However, even this possibility did not last long, as Arsenal were beaten 2-1 at home by future champions Manchester United five days later on 13 April. Fábregas played his fourth full game in eleven days and, despite some majestic moments in the Gunners' strong start, he faded badly in the second half as defensive vulnerability rocked the Londoners again. Adebayor put Arsenal ahead after 48 minutes but a Ronaldo penalty and a fine Hargreaves free-kick won the game for Manchester United. Fábregas' season was all but over.

Arsenal won their last four league games but it was all in vain as they finished in third place, two points behind Chelsea and four points behind Manchester United. Fábregas only played two of these last four games with Wenger giving a well-earned rest to his midfield playmaker. The Spaniard played full games against Reading and Derby but sat out Arsenal's final, ultimately meaningless games against Everton and Sunderland.

It was a sad end to an extremely promising season for Arsenal but Fábregas was at least rewarded in the end of season awards. Nominated for both PFA Player of the Year and PFA Young Player of the Year, Fábregas went on to win the latter award, as well as a place in the PFA Team of the Year.

Typically modest and generous in victory, the Spaniard dedicated the award to his team-mates: 'I am very proud because it is always satisfying for yourself, but all the team worked really hard this season and it's been disappointing at the end.'

The Spaniard finished the Premiership season with nine goals in 32 games, and most importantly 19 assists, the highest total in the league. A record of six goals and two assists in nine Champions League games was particularly impressive for a playmaker who had only just turned 21 and would surely only get better with age and experience.

As Wenger himself said: 'So long as he does not suffer any major injuries, he could certainly be the best midfielder in the world.'

Next up for Fábregas was the Euro 2008 Championships with Spain and a fight for a place in the starting eleven, against stiff competition from former Barcelona team-mates Xavi and Iniesta, as well as Senna and Xabi Alonso.

Before heading off for Austria and Switzerland, however, the Spaniard pledged his future to Arsenal, in the wake of growing interest from Inter Milan, Real Madrid and his former club Barcelona. Fábregas had only praise for his manager and was confident about next season. He told the press: 'I think we will win something, of course.'

CHAPTER 8

HIGHS AND LOWS AT HOME AND ABROAD

Cesc then switched his focus to the preparation for Euro 2008. The season had petered out for Arsenal but he had put that disappointment to one side. After all, the Spaniards felt they had a great chance of lifting the trophy in Austria and Switzerland.

Narrow wins in warm-up matches against Peru and USA did not mark Spain out as major threats but things were slowly coming together – and they did not want to reach their peak too early. Fábregas was full of hope. It was incredible to think that he was still so young and yet this was not his first international tournament. He had learnt a lot from Spain's premature exit in Germany in 2006 and hoped to be given the chance to make amends this time. Again, though, he was faced with the prospect of a place on the bench. It was no insult to be left out of one of the world's top midfields but Cesc knew he was good enough to command a starting role.

However, Aragones seemed to prefer using Xavi and

Senna in the centre of midfield with David Silva and Iniesta out wide. It meant that Spain were a little narrow at times but, with the rampaging runs of full-backs Sergio Ramos and Joan Capdevila, that was never a big concern.

Cesc watched on from the touchline as his team-mates walked out to face Russia in their opening fixture in Group D, which also featured Sweden and Greece. It promised to be a genuine test of Spain's tournament credentials with the Russians expected to offer a serious threat. In fact, some pundits had tipped Russia to be the Euro 2008 dark horses.

But Guus Hiddink's side were simply swept aside by a Spanish performance full of flair, pace and movement. Cesc had been disappointed not to make the starting line-up, however, he loved seeing the team playing so well. Villa was the star man, finishing brilliantly to bag a hat-trick as his partnership with Torres continued to blossom.

Fábregas entered the fray in the 54th minute for his European Championships debut. He instantly slotted into the team's patient passing style and helped leave the Russians floored. He capped a memorable afternoon in the closing moments by heading home Spain's fourth goal after Xavi's shot was parried – it was his first international goal. The game finished 4-1 and it was a big statement of intent – Spain meant business.

But, at the same time, it had the makings of an all too familiar story. So often, the Spaniards had flown out of the traps and looked on top form, only to slip to defeat in the knockout rounds. Cesc was determined that this year would be different and the mood in the dressing room after the win over Russia suggested that his team-mates felt the same way.

Cesc was given another second half cameo in Spain's second group match against Sweden. Unsurprisingly, Aragones was reluctant to tinker with a winning formula but this was a sterner test. The Swedes fell behind to a Torres goal but did not wilt like the Russians had. Instead, they levelled through Ibrahimovic.

Fábregas replaced Xavi with just over half an hour to go but found the Swedish rearguard tough to break down. It needed a last gasp Villa goal to snatch the points and leave Ibrahimovic and company stunned.

Cesc was delighted to be sitting in pole position in the group with six points out of six. It took the pressure off the final group game against Greece. He hoped that, as at the 2006 World Cup, the regulars would be rested for a meaningless game, allowing Fábregas and others to stake their claims for a starting berth.

Aragones did indeed rest the majority of his big guns and it gave Cesc a slot in midfield. Greece had nothing to play for but took the lead just before half-time. The Spanish second string had not clicked, yet a second half fightback earned a 2-1 win, with Ruben De la Red and Daniel Guiza on target. Guiza's winner came in the 88th minute. Fábregas was not at his best but hoped that there would be more opportunities ahead.

The excitement and glamour of the tournament left Fábregas speechless. A solid group stage was a big plus point but Spain had been equally stylish in 2006 and had been on the plane home after the second round. There would be no celebrations until the trophy was in the players' hands. Having topped the group, Fábregas and company progressed to face Italy. It promised to be a tough clash against the World Cup winners but there was a real sense of destiny in the Spanish squad. Cesc believed this was their year.

The quarter-final proved to be a dire affair and Fábregas had to watch from the substitutes' bench. The Italians made little effort to craft chances, keeping men behind the ball. With Spain making limited impact, Cesc was thrown into the action just before the hour mark and he attempted to kick-start the team's passing style. The 90 minutes finished goalless, as did extra-time. And so two of the nations with the worst penalty-taking records headed into a shootout.

Someone had to win, though, and Fábregas was determined that it would be Spain – so was Casillas. The Real Madrid stopper stole the show with penalty saves from Daniele De Rossi and Antonio Di Natale, leaving Spain needing to score their final penalty to be sure of a place in the semi-finals. And that fifth taker was Cesc.

Fábregas marched up to the spot and prepared for arguably the biggest moment of his career. And he kept his cool, slotting the kick past Buffon to spark huge celebrations. The Italians' approach had back-fired and Spain were now one match away from the final. Cesc had shown his character by putting his name forward for a spot-kick and seeing the penalty hit the back of the net was a feeling he would never forget.

He later admitted to the media that he had not taken a penalty in a match since he was 15 and that he had changed his plan for the spot-kick at the last minute. At the end of the day, it had worked for him – that was all that mattered.

The semi-finals paired Spain with Russia, who stunned Holland with a brilliant display of attacking football, in a group stage rematch. The rain poured down in Vienna and only one side came to the party. Fábregas started on the bench but entered the fray sooner than he could have possibly expected as Villa limped off. Cesc took up a role just behind Torres, prompting and looking for the killer pass.

The Russians had dazzled Holland with Andrei Arshavin to the fore but they surrendered limply in the second half against Fábregas and company. And it was Cesc who really lifted his team-mates and drove them to victory. He regularly found space to hurt the Russian back four and it was no surprise when Spain took a 50th-minute lead through Xavi.

Then Fábregas helped settle matters with a stunning pass for Guiza to double the lead. It was a pinpoint pass and summed up exactly what he brought to the team. And he was not finished yet. To rub salt into the Russians' wounds, he popped up with another fine assist as he laid on a third for Silva. Cesc had produced a play-making masterclass and the Spaniards were heading into the final. Their supporters sung 'Y Viva España' as the party began.

There was just one hurdle left in Fábregas' path. Germany had proved too strong for refreshingly spirited Turkey and it promised to be an entertaining finale to the tournament. Villa's injury was assessed and the news was bad for the striker – he was out of the final. So the big question was: would Aragones select Cesc in his place? It seemed a no-brainer as the midfielder had stolen all the headlines with his display against Russia. And Aragones agreed; Fábregas would start in the Euro 2008 final.

It had been a thrilling few weeks and now the Arsenal man had forced his way into the starting line-up for the biggest match of his career. The final began in cagey fashion but Spain quickly appeared to have the measure of their opponents and their pace in attack was frightening the German defence.

Fábregas found it hard to get into the match but was joining in the celebrations in the 33rd minute as Torres' pace and endeavour gave Spain a vital lead. The striker shrugged off Philipp Lahm and dinked the ball over the advancing Lehmann.

Cesc dug in to help his team-mates protect the lead, without managing to find the type of passes that had cut Russia to shreds. He was replaced by Alonso just after the hour mark and, though disappointed, he could reflect on a solid shift. Now, he would have to accept that he could not influence what happened next. Spain, who might have had Silva sent off, wasted several chances to extend the lead but the Germans could not make them pay.

When the final whistle went, it was mayhem. Fábregas and his team-mates had won their first major title for 44 years and they celebrated in style. There had been some brilliant performances throughout the tournament. Senna had been phenomenal as a defensive midfield screen, Torres and Villa had been lethal up front and Casillas had been inspired at times. And of course Cesc had chipped in with some fine work of his own along the way.

After the misery of walking past the Champions League trophy in 2006, Fábregas was ecstatic to be heading up for his winners medal and the chance to lift the big prize. He savoured the moment as Casillas raised the trophy and the celebrations carried on well into the night. The underachievers tag had been shed once and for all.

It had been a special summer but it meant Cesc had little time to rest. While the adrenalin rush of winning Euro 2008 would keep him going, it was not ideal for Wenger's plans to battle for silverware on four fronts. Fábregas did his best to recharge his batteries but then picked up an unfortunate hamstring injury that ruined his start to the campaign.

As the new season in England approached, Cesc again found himself dealing with some major changes. There had been speculation surrounding a number of the Arsenal players and this had been followed up with some concrete bids. Flamini was now an AC Milan player while Hleb completed a switch to Barcelona.

Having formed good chemistry with his fellow midfielders during the previous campaign, Fábregas now had to contemplate starting over with several new additions. Samir Nasri joined the Gunners from Marseille and would take over Hleb's role on the left flank.

But Cesc was left frustrated as his hamstring niggle forced him to miss out on pre-season. The Gunners entered the campaign with high hopes nonetheless and aimed to make a flying start. A home fixture against new boys West Brom appeared to be the perfect way for Arsenal to kick start their title bid as Fábregas watched on from the sidelines. Nasri put the Gunners ahead after just four minutes but the visitors shrugged off the setback and proved equal to Arsenal's best moments. Cesc was a relieved man at the final whistle to see his team-mates secure a 1-0 victory.

There was no doubt that his creative genius was missed in the centre of midfield. And the Gunners had to manage without their talisman for a few more weeks as he struggled to shake off the hamstring injury. While Arsenal had survived without him against West Brom, they were not so successful away to Fulham a week later.

A laborious and hopelessly uninspired performance at Craven Cottage saw Arsenal crash to a 1-0 defeat. There was no cutting edge and, worse still, no leadership. Fábregas had hoped that the squad had moved on from the days when they were outfought on their travels but this was a clear indication that the Gunners could still be bullied.

Cesc knew his team-mates needed his presence out on the field and worked hard to regain full fitness. He returned to the starting line-up in late August for the second leg against FC Twente as Arsenal won their Champions League qualifier and took their place in the group stage draw. It was an easy match and the perfect fixture in which to feel his way back to peak condition. This was Fábregas' first appearance since the Euro 2008 final and he played his part in a fine 4-0 victory.

It was no coincidence that Arsenal looked a brighter, more threatening side when Cesc was restored to the line-up. His range of passing and work ethic helped conjure a 3-0 win at home to Newcastle and then a 4-0 success at Blackburn two weeks later. Seven goals in two games was much more like the Arsenal of old.

A 1-1 draw in Kiev was a decent start to the Champions League group stage. Drawn alongside Dynamo Kiev, Fenerbahce and Porto, the Gunners were hot favourites to top the group but Fábregas was determined that the team would improve their away form in the process.

Further evidence of Cesc's impact on those around him came at Bolton on September 20. Arsenal fell behind to a Kevin Davies effort but showed the character to bounce back as Fábregas settled his team-mates and sparked their lightning passing approach. In the blink of an eye, Arsenal had turned things around and they held on for a 3-1 victory to move top of the table.

Having been afforded a rest in midweek while the club's young guns battered Sheffield United 6-0, Cesc returned to the side for the visit of Hull. Phil Brown's side had made a promising start to their first top flight campaign but man for man Arsenal looked vastly superior.

But on the day, it was Hull who rose to the occasion as Fábregas and his colleagues saw their title hopes suffer another blow. Despite taking the lead, Arsenal fell away and the Tigers pounced. Brazilian Geovanni fired in an unstoppable long range equaliser and Daniel Cousin completed the comeback with a fine header. Cesc was stunned. He knew the Gunners could not afford to throw away points at home.

The team bounced back in midweek with a 4-0 win over Porto. Fábregas was still looking for his first goal of the season and he went close with a testing 20-yard strike. The goals would come but he was desperate to emulate his prolific start to last season.

Sunderland provided the next challenge and the trip to the Stadium of Light would again test Arsenal's character on the road. The Black Cats had spent heavily over the summer and they swarmed all over Fábregas and company. With just four minutes to go, Sunderland struck a killer blow as Grant Leadbitter fired home a thunderbolt from just outside the area.

Arsenal might easily have been floored – but Cesc decided otherwise. He picked his team-mates up and pushed them forward. Then, from a late van Persie corner, Fábregas rose to head a dramatic late equaliser. The Gunners had barely deserved it but the Spaniard did not care as he celebrated jubilantly.

Three consecutive wins followed as Wenger's side began to find their feet again. Everton took the lead at the Emirates before Fábregas and his team-mates cruised through to a 3-1 victory. Arsenal then bagged five in Turkey against Fenerbahce and outlasted West Ham 2-0 on October 26.

But the Gunners just could not continue this consistency. Good spells of football were not rewarded with goals and defensive frailties started to show. And as much as anything, there did not seem to be any leadership on the pitch. Gallas was the captain yet he was not from the John Terry or Steven Gerrard school of motivation.

Despite taking charge of lengthy patches against Tottenham on October 29, Fábregas was left in dismay as a late Aaron Lennon finish earned Spurs an incredible 4-4 draw. For the neutrals, it was a classic. For the players and coaches, there was plenty to worry about. Cesc could not believe the team had given away a comfortable lead against a side who, after appointing Harry Redknapp to replace Juande Ramos, were only just beginning to put points on the board.

Worse followed at the weekend as Fábregas was part of another shocking away day performance. Travelling to

Stoke was always going to test how much backbone this Arsenal side possessed and they failed miserably. The Potters relied heavily on the menacing long throws of Rory Delap and the Gunners could not handle it.

Fábregas could not get into the game as Stoke chased and harried their way to a deserved 2-1 victory, with both goals coming from Delap's long bombs. It completed an infuriating week for Arsenal and left Cesc questioning the team's title chances. Until the team learned to win on their travels against more physical teams, they could forget about challenging Manchester United, Chelsea and Liverpool. It was a disturbingly familiar story for Fábregas.

Question marks continued to linger over Arsenal as they drew a blank in midweek at home to Fenerbahce. Again, the Gunners never really got into their stride despite some patches of stylish passing. Fábregas was involved in their best moves, setting up a great chance for van Persie. But the lack of an end product was once more the decisive factor for Wenger's side.

It was hardly the ideal way to prepare for a huge clash against Manchester United at the weekend. But, then again, Arsenal never had a problem getting motivated for the big games. It was the type of match that Fábregas loved and he knew he had to win his midfield duel with Michael Carrick and Anderson.

The rain poured down but the home fans at the Emirates got behind their team. And in the 22nd minute, they had something to really cheer as Nasri's fine strike was deflected in by Gary Neville. United, still adjusting to new signing Berbatov, threatened at the other end but the intensity and energy of Fábregas and company – that had been so badly lacking at Stoke – helped keep the champions at bay.

Cesc continued to pull the strings in the second half and, just three minutes after the break, Arsenal doubled their lead. Fábregas split the United defence with a clever pass, releasing Nasri to fire past van der Sar. By this stage, the atmosphere inside the Emirates was electric and the home supporters were desperate to celebrate a vital win.

But United young gun Rafael Da Silva came off the bench to pull a goal back with a fine left-footed effort, ensuring a nervy finale for Cesc and his team-mates. However, they held firm and the final whistle cued big celebrations. The players had needed this confidence boost and suddenly the league table looked a little less depressing. It had been a thrilling 90 minutes and Arsenal had edged it.

The youngsters won in the Carling Cup in midweek but Wenger brought back the big guns for the home fixture with Aston Villa on November 15. Hopes were high that Arsenal could kick on and Fábregas believed that there was plenty of life left in their title bid. Chelsea and Liverpool were looking strong but he fancied the Gunners' chances of turning them over at the Emirates.

Unfortunately for the Spaniard, the spirited victory over United proved to be a false dawn as Villa rocked the Emirates with a display full of pace and movement. This was supposed to be Arsenal's trademark but it was the likes of Gabriel Agbonlahor and Ashley Young who rose to the occasion.

And Fábregas could have no complaints. He had an effort well saved by Brad Friedel in the first half and could do nothing to prevent Villa outplaying the hosts. Young missed a penalty but Martin O'Neill's side took the points late-on as Clichy headed into his own net and Agbonlahor shrugged off Gallas to add a second.

Wenger was furious post-match. He said: 'It was a very bad afternoon because we were not sharp physically and beaten everywhere in the first half.' He also admitted to being frustrated that the three points against United had been wasted.

Then came more controversy as Gallas decided to air some his grievances publicly, hitting out about teams now being fearless when playing the Gunners and about the tensions behind the scenes. Just when Fábregas and company thought they had enough issues to deal with, the media picked up the story and the situation reached rock bottom.

Gallas told the Associated Press: 'There was a problem at half-time of the 4-4 draw with Tottenham. The only thing I could say at half-time was "guys, we resolve these problems after the match, not at half-time."

'When as captain some players come up to you and talk to you about a player... complaining about him... and then during the match you speak to this player and the player in question insults us, there comes a time where we can no longer comprehend how this can happen. I am trying to defend myself a bit without giving names. Otherwise I'm taking it all [the blame]. I'm 31, the player is six years younger than me.'

Cesc and his team-mates were stunned by the outburst and Wenger, who some felt ought to have been more decisive after some of Gallas' behaviour last season, was left with little choice but to take action. He dropped the French defender from the squad for the upcoming match at Manchester City and stripped him of the captaincy.

Lee Dixon supported the decision, telling the media: 'I think in the dressing room they're pleasantly surprised that Wenger has taken some action and not just sat back. Quite rightly, in my view, Arsene Wenger has acted on it.'

Fábregas was frustrated to be suspended for the trip to City. He wanted to be there to help his team-mates at this worrying time. Almunia captained the side but it was another afternoon to forget, wrapping up a disastrous week for Arsenal. Robinho, who had moved to Manchester for around £32.5 million in the summer, stole the show as City romped to a 3-0 victory.

It was a nightmare spell for everyone connected with the club but things picked up slightly for Cesc on the Monday as Wenger made his decision public on the vacant captain's armband.

He told reporters: 'Fábregas will be the captain permanently. I do not have to explain why. I believe the captain is the voice of the club towards the outside, and is one of the leaders of the team.'

While there was not as much cause for celebration due to Arsenal's recent failings, this was a huge moment for Cesc. He had arrived in London hoping to establish himself as a professional footballer and now he was the Gunners' captain.

The Spaniard told the club's website: 'It is a great honour for me to captain one of the biggest clubs in the world. It is a proud moment. I know it's a big responsibility but together with my team-mates, I know we have the spirit and commitment to get back to winning ways and fulfil our potential.'

Arsenal's future was now very much in Fábregas' hands. It would not change his playing style particularly but his team-mates would turn to him more than ever. He was ready for the challenge and hoped to make his manager proud.

A home fixture against Dynamo Kiev was just what Cesc and company needed. It appeared to be a relatively easy match and the home crowd would be eager to welcome their new captain. But confidence was at such a low ebb that it was a major struggle. Fábregas led the way with a man of the match performance but Arsenal needed an 87th minute winner from Bendtner, who was picked out superbly by Cesc, to snatch the win.

His spell as captain had begun with a win and this was the most important thing for the Gunners at present. Things would get harder before they got easier, though, because next on their fixture list was a trip to Stamford Bridge to face Chelsea. But Fábregas has never been one to shirk a challenge and he could not wait to lead his team out in such a massive fixture. It would be a true test of his ability to motivate those around him.

Arsenal have never struggled to raise their game for the big matches and they once again proved this point with a gutsy performance at Stamford Bridge. Fábregas was industrious in midfield but Chelsea dictated play and took the lead when Djourou diverted the ball into his own net.

It was a real blow but Cesc ensured that his team-mates did not panic. They were struggling to find any rhythm going forward yet the longer it stayed at 1-0, the more hope there was of crafting an equaliser. Then, in three incredible second half minutes, the Gunners turned the match on its head as van Persie struck twice to silence Stamford Bridge.

His first appeared comfortably offside but the flag did not go up and Arsenal were level. Cesc implored his team-mates to kick on and the Dutchman did the business again in the 62nd minute as he turned and fired a left-footed shot into the bottom corner. Fábregas, leading by example, harried and chased for the final half hour and the Blues quickly became frustrated. When the final whistle went, he joined in the celebrations. After all the off-field drama, this was the perfect response.

The youngsters went out of the Carling Cup in midweek but the next weekend saw the Gunners build on the win at Chelsea with a 1-0 victory over Wigan thanks to an Adebayor strike. Maybe Arsenal were finally finding the necessary consistency.

However, a defeat to Porto in the Champions League consigned the Gunners to second place in the group and a potentially tougher second round match. Then a trip to Middlesbrough reminded everyone that Fábregas and company still had plenty of improvements to make. Adebayor headed the side into the lead but Jeremie Aliadiere levelled and the Gunners dropped two more frustrating points.

The Spaniard had been going about his business quietly and efficiently as always but the team were not looking as imposing without the likes of Hleb and Flamini. Cesc knew he needed to contribute more goals from midfield but felt pleased with his general form.

However, just as Fábregas was looking ahead to the rest of the season, disaster struck. Arsenal clashed with Liverpool at the Emirates on 21 December. Benitez's side were looking genuine title contenders but Cesc and company wanted to knock them out of their stride. Van Persie gave the Gunners the lead before Robbie Keane pulled the visitors level. But, just before half-time, Fábregas and Alonso challenged for a loose ball in a tackle that left the Arsenal skipper writhing in agony. He was helped off the field at the break and would not return.

The news was extremely bad for all associated with the Gunners. Fábregas would miss up to four months with ruptured knee ligaments. It left Cesc and Arsenal shattered. The talisman was out of action and the new era, with the Spaniard running the show, was suddenly on hold. He told the press: 'It's the first serious injury that I've had in my career. Everyone gets injured and now it's my turn. My intention is to return as soon as possible to help my team-mates and to do what I like most, to play football.'

The outcome of Arsenal's season would largely depend on how Fábregas' team-mates could rally themselves in his absence. Could they find consistency? On their day, they were capable of beating anyone – just ask Manchester United and Chelsea – but Cesc was all too aware that plenty of sloppy points had already been surrendered. He would return for the final stretch of the season but he would have to wait and see whether there would be any trophies still to play for.

CHAPTER 9

THE YEARS AHEAD

Few players on the planet can look forward to a more exciting future than Fábregas. He and Manchester United's Cristiano Ronaldo appear set to dominate the Premiership for years to come – and no doubt the international stage, too. Cesc seems to have been around for ages; on television, in the newspapers, in magazines. Yet he only has five years in the Arsenal first team under his belt and it is remarkable to think that he is still so young.

Cesc is under no illusions, though. He continues to strive to improve his game and works as hard as ever in training. The Spaniard is still learning and would happily admit that he is not yet the finished product. Having said that, if he keeps developing at the current rate, Fábregas will hit the heights earlier than anticipated. The last two years have lifted him into an elite group of footballers around the world who can rightly claim to be special talents.

Refreshing for Wenger and all Gunners fans is the fact that Cesc appears committed to the Arsenal cause for the foreseeable future. There have been reports linking the Spaniard with a move back to his homeland, but Fábregas has shrugged these off with the same assurance with which he eludes most Premiership opponents and he has stated his love for the club on numerous occasions. It is hardly surprising, considering that Arsenal were the team to give Cesc the chance to become a professional. He is now keen to pay back the faith the club has shown in him by taking the Gunners back to the glory days.

This is a very important part of Fábregas' vision for the future. What Wenger has been building at Arsenal is not simply a team to compete for the title in the short term, but a group of players who can carry the club forward for the next decade. Cesc wants to lead the side through this exciting era. The emphasis on bringing youngsters through into the first team as soon as possible has always been designed to secure the Gunners' future success.

Looking at the Arsenal squad, it is clear that Wenger has done a good job. While Cesc is the outstanding member of the group, there are plenty of other class acts. Adebayor and van Persie have youth on their side, as does Eduardo. The list goes on and includes fledglings Denilson, Armand Traoré and Nicklas Bendtner. There is every chance that Cesc will be part of an exciting Arsenal dynasty. This prospect will surely have occurred to Fábregas as he contemplated joining Real Madrid or Barcelona and may well have persuaded him to devote himself to Wenger's long-term plans.

Had the Frenchman not signed a contract extension, though, Cesc might well be playing in the Bernabeu for

Real by now. Such is the regard with which Fábregas holds Wenger, confirmation that his manager was staying was enough to sway the midfielder into committing to the club himself. Arsène has been like a father figure for Cesc since the day the Spaniard first arrived at the club as a sixteen-year-old and must take plenty of the credit for the way he has matured into such a complete player.

Cesc has established himself as a firm favourite with the Gunners fans and in their eyes he can do no wrong. In the early days, their support helped him to settle into the first team and Fábregas looks forward to giving them plenty more special moments, strengthening the bond that they share by winning the top prizes at home and abroad.

His contract at the Emirates currently runs until 2014, ensuring that the midfielder spends many more years crafting chances for the likes of Adebayor, Eduardo and van Persie. To have Cesc's creativity in the side is a striker's dream as the Spaniard prides himself on assists in the same way that front men regard goals. Fábregas has the eye for a killer pass and all three of the Arsenal forwards have the pace to profit from through balls behind opposition defences.

There is still so much more for the Spaniard to achieve at Arsenal. His first three seasons yielded just an FA Cup winners medal, whetting his appetite for more silverware. But there has been nothing since at club level. While these were admittedly only his formative years in professional football, Fábregas was not content and hopes are high that more success will follow. Losing the Champions League final in 2006 has only strengthened his desire to return to such a big occasion and end up as a winner. It would certainly take a very brave man to bet against him doing so at some point in his career.

With the maturity he has shown this season, Fábregas seems likely to be Arsenal's captain for years to come. He has displayed the right qualities since being handed the armband, taking on responsibility in tight matches and leading by example in midfield. So often it has been Cesc who has lifted his team-mates when their levels have dropped. He certainly has the respect and admiration of his team-mates and has been immaculately behaved since arriving in London in 2003. He is a good role model for youngsters and would be an excellent representative for the club. Fábregas might also captain his country one day – though there are plenty of other young candidates in the Spanish squad.

There will, of course, be plenty more big tournaments ahead for Cesc. Like Cristiano Ronaldo, there is every reason to think that Fábregas will appear in the World Cups of 2010, 2014 and 2018, as well as the European Championships of 2012, 2016 and maybe even 2020. By starting out as a youngster in international football, he has given himself every opportunity to enjoy a long and successful career. It will be a proud time for Barcelona as Cesc, Iniesta and Xavi – all products of the Nou Camp *cantera* – continue to spearhead Spanish bids at major tournaments over the next decade. There are few European nations who can look forward to such a bright future and even fewer that could boast an equally talented midfield.

Even at this early stage in his career, it seems inevitable that the youngster will eventually return to Spain. More than once he has referred to this possibility when addressing the media and in October 2007 he admitted: 'For everybody it is a dream to play for one of the big clubs in Spain when you are Spanish.' Barcelona have always been the club closest to his heart; the club that made him as a footballer. While Fábregas is currently loving life at the Emirates, the prospect of a move to Barça in the years ahead might well prove too attractive for him to turn down.

It is a scary thought for opposition teams that Fábregas could link up again with his *cantera* colleagues Messi, Xavi and Iniesta one day. Being closer to his family and friends would be another benefit of heading back to Spain. It seems likely that Fábregas will one day grace the Nou Camp as a Barcelona player and, as long as it is not too soon, it would be hard for Arsenal fans to begrudge him something that has been a lifelong dream.

Would he ever consider playing for Real Madrid, considering the history between Real and Barcelona? It is tough to say. Would the Barça fans ever forgive such treachery? Unlikely. But it is impossible to rule out such a move. On numerous occasions, reports have circulated suggesting that a switch to the Bernabeu was imminent for Cesc. None of them have materialised, despite the best efforts of the Real directors and managers. It is certainly flattering for Cesc to hear reports suggesting that the two biggest clubs in Spain are fighting for his signature. So far he has managed to resist the temptation to swap the wind and rain of England for sunnier climes.

La Liga is an obvious draw for Fábregas, but he remains motivated by the challenges of the Premiership: 'In England, I think it's the most competitive – technically, tactically, physically.' Yet he added: 'Without doubt there is more quality in Spain.' However, this does not mean that Cesc is ruling out remaining at Arsenal for the rest of his career. An article in the *Evening Standard* in November 2007 quoted the Spaniard as saying: 'Look at [Patrick] Vieira, [Thierry] Henry, Ray Parlour, Martin Keown. These kind of players have been here all their life. Look at Raul in Spain. Xavi and [Carlos] Puyol for Barcelona. They have played all their life for the same club.' There was nothing strange about that for him.

Still years away from reaching his peak as a player, the sky is indeed the limit for Fábregas. He does not, though, possess the patience to wait for silverware and that could be the key to how long he stays at Arsenal. A footballer of Cesc's calibre ought to be competing for domestic and European honours year in, year out. Wenger knows the Gunners must deliver on the big stage if they hope to keep the same personnel over the coming seasons. The clock is ticking.

In many ways, Fábregas is torn over his feelings for Spain and England. He insists that he will always be Spanish through and through, but admits that he has taken London to his heart since his move to the English capital. He has even admitted: 'I wouldn't mind if my son or sons were English.' The fact he can see himself at Arsenal that far down the line is a promising sign.

Away from football, Fábregas has always been happy to throw himself into charity work. While his presence at children's hospitals or care homes is met with a frenzied reception, Cesc gets just as much enjoyment out of such days himself. He has always felt privileged to be a professional footballer and to earn such huge sums of money. He knows how lucky he is to be doing what he loves for a living, but he does not act as though this makes him any better than anyone else.

This is one of the most refreshing aspects of Fábregas' character: his reluctance to accept his star status. He remains very modest and tries to avoid the limelight in a manner that is rather reminiscent of Paul Scholes. This attitude allows him to slot easily into his old life in Barcelona when he returns to the city and his friends appreciate the fact that fame has not gone to his head. He is still the same Cesc they knew at school and on the local football pitches. These friendships are part of the reason why Fábregas is able to keep his feet on the ground. His mates do not treat him any differently – apart from their keen interest in the ins and outs of life in the Premiership.

Charity projects allow him to give something back to the public and the Spaniard loves to discuss football with Gunners supporters. TreeHouse, which helps children with autism, and Arsenal have joined forces to raise money and Fábregas and his team-mates have been involved in the scheme, spending days with the children and giving funding to help with the running of the centres. While some players might find these commitments a chore, Cesc has never felt that way. It is not in his character. Invariably, you will see him interacting with the children – a beaming smile all over his face. Fábregas does not expect thanks for his involvement as he sees it as part of his job as a role model and he takes great pride in brightening up the youngsters' days. It seems very likely that the Spaniard will continue to support such charities after he decides to bring an end to his playing days.

Retirement will allow him the freedom to meet up

with his friends in Spain more often and see his family on a regular basis. The tight regulations on his diet, put in place by Wenger, will be relaxed and Fábregas will be able to eat what he likes again without worrying about his weight and fitness. He can devour all the Krispy Kreme doughnuts he wants without the slightest trace of guilt!

One of the biggest benefits of being a professional footballer in this modern era is that the high wages paid to players ensure their financial futures. By the time Cesc thinks about retirement, he will have played in excess of fifteen seasons and his earnings will leave him with plenty of options when he comes to making big decisions.

Would management appeal to him? Would he consider a career in punditry in England or in Spain? It would be tough to imagine Cesc walking away from the game altogether – after all, it has given him so many special memories already. Having played under Wenger, Fábregas will be well placed to move into a coaching role – after all, Arsène's attention to detail has always been phenomenal. The Frenchman has been pivotal in Cesc's development and no doubt the Spaniard has picked up plenty of valuable tips that he could use if he went into management himself. There are few better role models than Wenger for young coaches.

As with all high-profile sportsmen, Fábregas has attracted plenty of interest from top brands looking to agree sponsorship deals. It is tricky for youngsters to make the right decisions in this regard and Cesc has been fortunate that he has always received good advice from those around him. His contract with Nike is certainly lucrative and he can be seen in television adverts and in magazines modelling the brand – whether it is football boots, training kit or other merchandise. There will certainly be no end of interest from sponsors if Fábregas continues to shine. The big concern will be over choosing the offers that suit him best and protect his interests.

It is safe to say, though, that he will not follow David Beckham and former Gunner Freddie Ljungberg into modelling underwear. Naturally shy, Fábregas would not be spotted taking part in semi-naked photo shoots. Cesc prefers to stay away from controversy and Wenger has been fortunate in that regard – Cesc has never given him the sorts of problems that more reckless young footballers have brought upon their managers.

Instead, Fábregas prefers the quiet life and will look to settle down with his girlfriend, Carla, in years to come. The pair have overcome the difficulties that often beset long-distance relationships and seem set to wed. So long as Cesc stays at Arsenal, the couple will, in all likelihood, choose to live in London together. Carla is one of the influences in Fábregas' life that helps to keep his feet firmly on the ground, though the midfielder has admitted that she will not tolerate him watching the endless stream of televised matches when they are at home.

That is one of the ways that he likes to relax – either watching live games or re-runs of games in which he has played. Like his manager, Cesc finds it tough to switch off from the sport. He also enjoys watching US shows such as *Desperate Housewives* and *Lost* as a way to unwind and forget about football for a short while.

With the pressures of life as a high-profile Premiership player, it is important for Fábregas to find a way of occupying himself away from the game. The wages received by the top stars are so high that it is always a concern the money might go to the heads of those just starting out in the league. Fortunately for Wenger, Fábregas has always had interests outside of football and his relationship with Carla is a perfect way for Cesc to remember the bigger picture – the world does not revolve around football.

Carla came over from Spain to study in London during the 2005/06 season and it helped Fábregas greatly to have her support. After all the time spent apart, it made a change for the pair to be together for a long stretch. At the end of her year in England, she had to return to Spain to finish her studies, but has since come back to London to live with Cesc. It gives him the right balance in his private life and this happiness makes him a brighter, more cheerful individual.

Fábregas has a strong relationship with his family too, as he explained in an interview with the *Guardian* in August 2007: 'I don't need to tell my family when I feel bad because they see straightaway how I feel. They are my parents and so, because I'm still young, they are the first ones I turn to whether I'm happy or sad. My girlfriend knows that as well. As soon as they see my face they know how I am on the inside. I talk to them after four hours, when the bad feelings have gone and I am calmer.'

Whatever the distant future might hold, it is the next few years that will be most interesting as the Spaniard strives to fill his trophy cabinet. Fábregas has already established himself as a top-class footballer, but wants to go on to win the prizes that other star names have earned.

During the 2007/08 season, Sir Alex Ferguson told the media that Cesc could only be called a 'great' player when he had the silverware to prove it and Fábregas took note. The Spaniard told *The Sunday Times*: 'I 100 percent agree with him [Ferguson]. I can't say I'm a great player. And I always say at Arsenal we're a very, very good side, but not a great side. When we win something together as a group we can say we're great. You've been successful when you've won trophies. When you've won European Championships, World Cups, Premier Leagues, Champions Leagues: then you can say you're a success.'

That would be quite a collection, but if anyone has the talent and desire to win all those trophies during their career, it is Fábregas.

ACKNOWLEDGEMENTS

I would like to thank Nick Callow and the staff at Hayters Teamwork for their guidance and encouragement. I am also indebted to the efficient work of Allie Collins and Lucian Randall at John Blake Publishing.

Similarly, I am very thankful for the input and advice of Phillip Buckley and the team at www.insidefutbol.com.

As always, I am eternally grateful to my friends, family and fiancée Melissa for their understanding and support. Thank you.

Further mention should go to Chauncey Billups' Detroit Pistons – and now Denver Nuggets – and to Lee Child for providing healthy distractions during the writing process.